HERTFORDSHIRE C

ABOUT THE SOCIETY

The East Herts Footpath Society is a Registered Charity (no. 1008960) and is affiliated to The Open Spaces Society and The Ramblers' Association.

The Society was founded in 1970 with the objects of protecting access to the countryside on foot and of encouraging interest in the countryside. As part of its activities, it organises regular guided walks in Hertfordshire and elsewhere.

The Society also opposes the closure of footpaths and seeks enforcement of the laws which should ensure that all public paths are signposted and free from obstructions.

If you would like to know more about the Society please contact the Membership Secretary:

Ray Turner
81 St Margaret's Road
Stanstead Abbots
WARE
SG12 8ER

ABOUT THIS BOOK

The walks described in this book have been devised as a chain of linking circular walks which stretch from near Crews Hill Station in the London Borough of Enfield to Ashwell & Morden Station in Cambridgeshire. Each walk is complete in itself and finishes at its starting point. In order to combine two or more walks, linking points have been shown in the maps which appear at the head of each walk description, so that the really ambitious can walk from London to Cambridgeshire (and back!) in this way.

The Society is indebted to a large number of people who have given freely of their time and services to make this book possible. Following conception of the series of walks, volunteers spent a great deal of time planning the routes, which were then walked and re-walked as necessary. The walk descriptions then had to be typed and the maps and sketches drawn. We are grateful to Jack Edwards for writing the Foreword and to the Hertfordshire Museum and County Record Office for permission to reproduce illustrations.

Hertfordshire Chain Walk

15 Linked Walks Through Rural East Hertfordshire

SECOND EDITION

Published for

East Herts Footpath Society

by

Castlemead
PUBLICATIONS
WELWYN GARDEN CITY

First Published in 1987

Second Edition 1994

CASTLEMEAD PUBLICATIONS
12 Little Mundells
Welwyn Garden City
Herts AL7 1EW

Proprietors:
WARD'S PUBLISHING SERVICES

ISBN 0 948555 36 X

© East Herts Footpath Society 1994

British Library Cataloguing in Publication Data
A catalogue record for this book is available from the
British Library

Phototypeset in $^{10}/_{11}$ Ehrhardt Roman
by Intype, London
Printed and bound in Great Britain
by The Burlington Press (Cambridge) Ltd

FOREWORD

Footpaths have been important since earliest times, their rights of way jealously guarded by the ordinary people. They existed to link the remoter hamlets – the Ends and Greens – of parishes with churches, their inns, and shops and with the nearest markets. Hence paths over-spilled into neighbouring parishes and, as this book demonstrates, it is possible to walk by footpath from the south to the north of Hertfordshire.

In this century when most of us have forsaken the exercise of walking for the speed and comfort of the motor car, the ancient ways are used mainly by enthusiastic ramblers. Bodies like the East Herts Footpath Society, who have cleared many cluttered paths and make representations on the public's behalf to keep paths open, are to be commended.

To all lovers of our beautiful Hertfordshire and of the healthy activity of walking, I have pleasure in recommending this book.

Jack Edwards
(*Local Historian*)
February 1987

Queen Hoo Hall (south view) — Buckler 1832

CONTENTS

ROAD SAFETY

Most of the walks in this book involve some walking on motor roads. Remember the Highway Code rules for pedestrians:-

1. Where there is a pavement or footpath, use it. Where possible, avoid walking next to the kerb with your back to the traffic. If you have to step into the road, watch out for traffic.

2. Where there is no pavement or footpath, walk on the right-hand side of the road so that you can see oncoming traffic. Keep close to the side of the road. Take care at sharp right-hand bends; it may be safer to cross the road well before you reach one so that oncoming traffic has a better chance of seeing you. After the bend cross back to face the oncoming traffic. Walk in single file if possible, especially on narrow roads or in poor light.

3. Wear or carry something that will help you to be seen. Light-coloured, bright or fluorescent items will help in poor visibility.

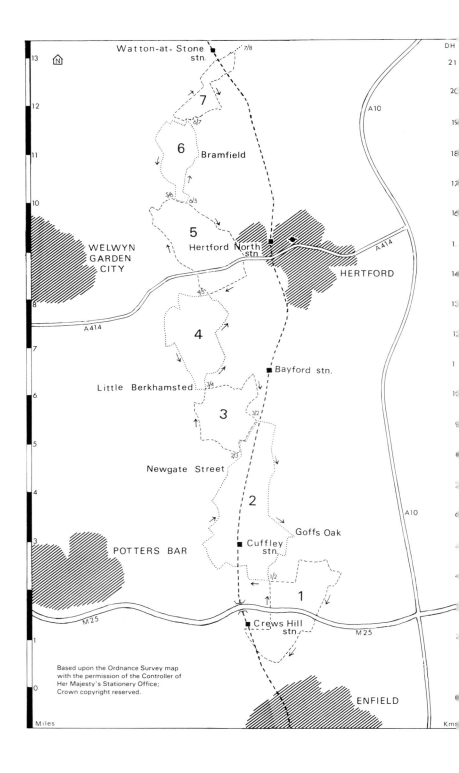

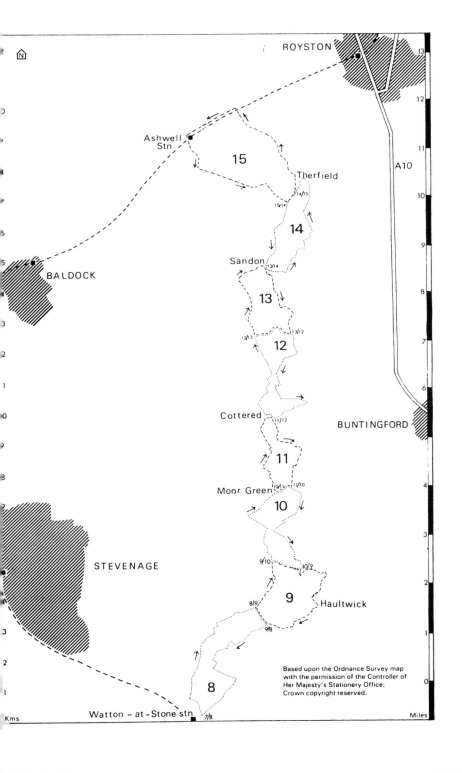

REPORTING PATH PROBLEMS

At the back of this book, we have reproduced the Countryside Commission's Access Charter. This gives you a brief summary of your rights and responsibilities out in the country. The local highway authority has a duty to assert and protect the rights of the public to the use and enjoyment of all public paths.

The highway authority for all paths in Hertfordshire is the County Council. In some parts of the county, its functions are carried out by District Councils acting as agents, but the responsibility still rests ultimately with the County Council. In future, local government reorganisation may change this pattern but, at present, the address for all reports of problems encountered on Hertfordshire paths is:

> Countryside Access Service
> Planning and Environment Department
> County Hall
> HERTFORD
> SG13 8DN
> (0992) 555236

Please give as much information as you can when reporting problems: the date, the place (including OS grid reference), the nature of the problem and the name of any landowner or occupier you obtained. If the path is one in this book then quote chapter and verse to the County Council, which will have a copy of the book.

Hertfordshire County Council has produced a Citizen's Charter to set goals for the services which it provides. To protect access to the countryside, the Council 'will aim to trace and contact landowners about obstructions on public rights of way within 14 days of notification and if necessary start enforcement action within six weeks'. The Council also aims to provide a substantive answer to all enquiries within 14 days.

The East Herts Footpath Society would be grateful for any feedback you can give on how the Council lives up to these promises. Please send any information or comments on this book to the Secretary:

> Mark Westley
> Little Hollies
> 38 Shephall Green
> STEVENAGE
> SG2 9XS

WALK NO. 1

Whitewebbs Park to Crews Hill

Whitewebbs Park – Crews Hill – Woodgreen Farm – Broadfield Farm – Whitewebbs Park

Distance 7 miles

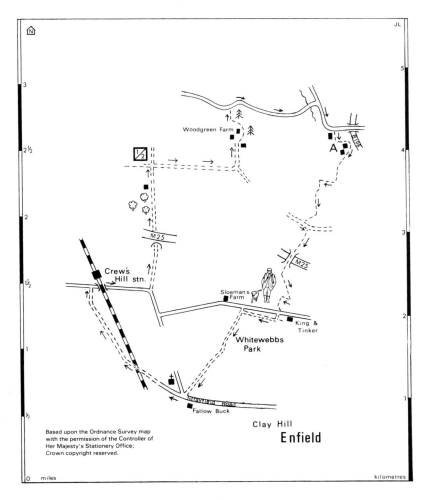

Park in Whitewebbs Road just west of the 'King and Tinker' public house (GR 329998). Crews Hill Station is just over a mile from this point and is on the route of this walk.

This walk starts in Whitewebbs Road in the London Borough of Enfield, alongside the boundary fence of Whitewebbs Park, just west of the King and Tinker public house.

We now describe the route along the road because Whitewebbs Park is not always open. A route through the Park is preferable and you could proceed inside the Park along a bridlepath that runs parallel to the road. Go along the road for 500 yards passing two entrances to Whitewebbs Park on your left. Turn left along a bridleway. Make this left turn before you reach Sloemans Farm which you can see to your right. This is a wide bridleway through the Park but it is usually muddy. You may prefer to use the path in the Park just beyond the fence on your left. Continue downhill until you cross a stream then proceed uphill. Further on uphill the bridleway becomes narrower. Keep straight on until you reach the road where you emerge opposite the Fallow Buck public house. Cross the road and turn right to proceed along Strayfield Road (a 'No Through Road'), passing the church on your right.

Walk northwestwards along Strayfield Road. You pass Astley House on your right. Keep straight on where the road becomes a gravel track at the Enfield Borough 'No Vehicles' sign. Keep straight on through a gateway. The path goes gradually uphill. Continue over a stile and along a narrow path with railings on both sides. Go downhill to cross the railway and then uphill along the path on the other side.

Straight on over a stile through a wooded section. You have woods on the right and a golf course on the left. Straight on along a grassy track where you have the golf course on both sides. Remain on this track and eventually it bears a little to the right as you approach the club house. At the club house bear slightly right and cross the car park to emerge onto the road. There, cross to the far side and turn right along the pavement and pass under the bridge at Crews Hill Station.

Continue with garden centres on both sides and, shortly after the Plough public house, where the road turns sharply right, you turn left into a lane with a board advertising 'Glasgow Stud', which you follow under the M25, entering Hertfordshire as you do so. Further along you pass a quaint cottage on your left. You proceed slightly uphill until you come to a junction of tracks 1/2 and there you turn right.

You are still on a wide gravel lane. The lane goes over a rise, crosses a large ditch and then continues uphill. When you reach the junction of tracks turn left. You pass under electricity wires close to a pole on your left which carries wires going in three directions. This is a wide gravel track with a hedge on the left and field on the right. Pass under the electricity wires. Go through a gateway and bear right at Woodgreen

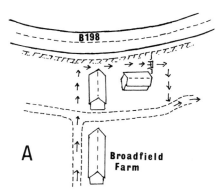

A   Broadfield Farm

Farm. At a junction of tracks a few yards distant bear left and proceed between farm buildings. After the farm remain on the track, which has a couple of bends, until you reach the road (Silver Street) and there turn right.

Continue on the road to the T-junction with Halstead Hill, where there is a letter box. Turn right. Pass a 'left bend' road sign. Around the left bend, and just after you pass the last house on your right, turn right along a footpath with the boundary of the house on your right. In a little more than 100 yards, at the junction of tracks turn left. Pass under electricity wires. Pass a power pole on your left where the wires terminate. Proceed along a track with farm buildings on your right. At a T-junction with a concrete track cross over and keep straight on. In a few yards, just before you reach the fence overlooking the dual carriageway, turn right (*see* sketch A). In another few yards you climb over a stile beside an iron gate in front of you and turn right. Cross a grassy area to reach a gravel track and there turn left.

Pass through another gateway. You are going downhill walking directly away from farm buildings behind you and moving further away from the main road to your left. Cross a wide wooden bridge over a ditch. Keep straight ahead over a stile beside an iron gate into a field and immediately turn right. In a few yards turn left, going uphill with the field on your left and the hedge on your right. The hedge peters out on your right but there is a line of trees. At the corner of the field cross a fence and immediately turn right so you continue with a hedge on your right and the field on your left. There are electricity wires in the field on your left.

At the corner of this field turn left and pass a power pole with double insulators on your right. You now have the field on your left and a wood on your right. After following the edge of the wood for a quarter of a mile, cross an earth bridge over a ditch and then turn right. Continue with a field on your left and the wood still on your right. Where the wood ends you have buildings on your left. Pass under electricity wires and close to old sheds and buildings on your left. You soon reach a gravel track and there turn left onto Oldpark Ride.

In about 80 yards you turn right just before a 'Private No Footpath' sign. (The section of gravel track which you have just used is a public right of way).

You are on a grassy track with an open field on both sides aiming for the left end of a plantation. There is a view of London ahead. Cross the M25 on a concrete footbridge. You are now leaving Hertfordshire and entering the London Borough of Enfield. Keep straight on along a grassy path which has fields on both sides. Pass under electricity wires with a pylon to your right. Descend to a stile which you cross, go over a bridge and continue in the same direction with the field to your left and a hedge and fence on your right to another stile.

At the corner of the next field cross the stile and turn right along a narrow path between hedges and fences. In just over 50 yards turn left along a path which is muddy and has fences on both sides. Stay on this path until you emerge onto the road (Whitewebbs Lane) opposite the King and Tinker public house. (You will have to cross a sequence of stiles). Turn right along Whitewebbs Road to return to the start of the walk.

The King and Tinker Inn — c.1884

WALK NO. 2

Goff's Oak to Newgate Street Village

Goff's Oak – Cuffley – Newgate Street Village – Wormley Wood – Goff's Oak

Distance 9 miles

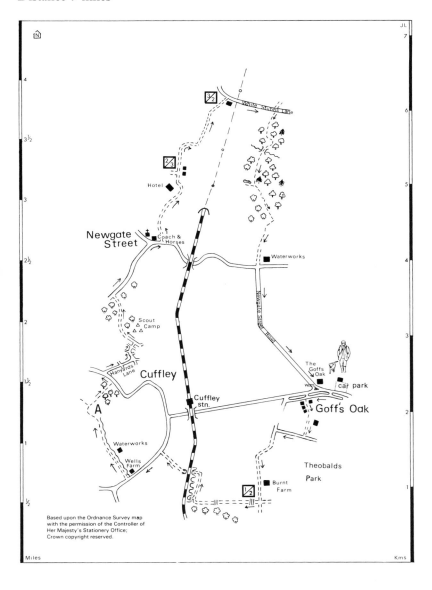

There is a public car park in front of Goff's Oak Library which is entered from Goff's Lane 100 yards to the east of the War Memorial. A pedestrian right of way emerges alongside the Post Office which is a few paces from the War Memorial. Cuffley Station is 1 mile west of this point down Cuffley Hill.

This walk starts at the bottom of Newgatestreet Road, Goff's Oak, by the war memorial. Cross the main road and then turn right along the service road. Turn left at the footpath which is adjacent to house number 27. You will reach a bushy area. Keep left following a garden boundary fence on your left. The path becomes narrower and you have bushes or fences on both sides. You pass close to houses on your right, where there is a wooden garden fence, and on your left there is a hedge. Keep straight on through an area of brambles. Bear slightly left at a junction of grassy tracks where you have a big house further to your right. Proceed with a wooden fence on your right and another fence on your left. Next you have barbed wire on your right and a hedge on your left. Keep straight on where there are wooden gates on both sides.

Cross a stile and proceed straight on uphill. Cross another stile to emerge onto a tarmac drive. Keep straight on and pass under electricity wires. At the junction with the road turn right. Keep straight on along the road ignoring stiles into the playing fields on your right. At the T-junction of roads turn left along Jones Road.

Good views here. Keep straight on where there is a gateway and the surface changes from tar to gravel. Pass under electricity wires. The track goes down into a dip then up again and at the brow of the hill you pass a farm (Burnt Farm) on your left. Keep straight on until you reach a crossing of tracks. 1/2

Turn right here to cross the cattle grid and continue on a gravel track with open fields on both sides towards a distant railway viaduct. Keep straight on where the track goes downhill and pass through a wide gap in the hedgerow. Continue on a level gravel track with open fields on both sides. You reach another cattle grid that forms a bridge over a stream and there are woods close on your left. Cross the stream and continue straight on with woods on your left and the railway viaduct ahead. Where the woods on your left cease turn right, to stay on the track.

In 40 yards there is a junction of tracks. The main track makes a turn to the left but you continue straight ahead across a concrete bridge, walking parallel to the railway viaduct which you see to your left. The track goes uphill with open fields on both sides. In the middle of the field turn left where the track curves left. This turn is well before you reach the big pylon. At the edge of the field keep straight on to pass through an arch under the railway.

When you emerge from the tunnel, bear slightly right where the path has fields on both sides. Pass under the electricity wires. Keep straight

6

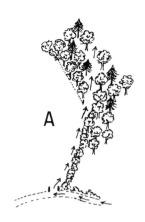

on through a gateway onto a path with hedges on both sides until you pass through an iron gateway to emerge onto the main road (Northaw Road East). Turn left.

The road goes downhill and near the bottom you pass Wells Farm on the right. Cross a small bridge over a stream and then immediately turn right. Continue on a footpath where there is an open field on your left and a ditch on your right. This starts as a concrete track and then becomes a gravel track. Cross a stile alongside a gate and then continue straight on. Go through a gateway where you have a pair of houses and water works buildings on your right.

Keep straight on with an open field on your left and the ditch on your right. Go through another gateway and cross a concrete bridge over a ditch, pass under electricity wires and keep straight on. Stay on this track as it curves to the left. Soon after that left bend there is an opening on the right.

Make a sharp right turn there so that you continue with an open field on your left and a hedge on your right (*see* sketch A). As you proceed uphill look carefully for the point where the path enters the woods on your right. You may have the impression that this is a right turn, but the path is really straight on and it is the boundary of the woods which curves. Continue uphill on a fairly well-defined path in a wooded area. Stay on this path which goes uphill and becomes narrower. The woods lie mainly to your left and you are close to the boundary on your right. Cross a stile to emerge onto a road (The Ridgeway) and turn left.

Turn right when you reach Hanyards Lane just before the '40 mph' speed limit signs. Keep straight on where Bradgate joins on the left. Turn left at Hill Rise. Straight on at Woodview. Bear right where Warwick Avenue joins on the left. Straight on where Farm Close joins on the right. At the T-junction turn left into Tolmers Road.

Pass Tolmers Scout Camp entrance on your right and continue straight on along a lane. Where the lane ends keep straight on through a gate along a gravel path entering woodlands. Keep straight on uphill, ignoring a minor path on the left. Continue on this fairly well-defined path through the woods, which has a fence on the right-hand side, until you reach the road (Carbone Hill) and there turn right. The road goes steeply uphill and you continue until you reach Newgate Street Village. There turn right opposite the Coach and Horses public house.

In little more than 50 yards turn left along a public bridleway which is the drive to Ponsbourne Park. The path has a tarred surface and goes downhill. The path rises again and you pass Ponsbourne Park on your left. Continue straight on along a gravel track. At the junction keep straight on, ignoring the path to the right. Veer slightly left, ignoring another path to the right. Pass tennis courts on your left then, as the path veers left, you pass silos on your right. The path then curves to the right and continues alongside a high, ornamental, brick wall.

Keep straight on past a pair of cottages on your left and then houses on your right. 2/3 Where you have a power pole ahead stay on the track and pass under the electricity wires where the track turns right. Pass a pond on your right and soon after that make a left turn to stay on the gravel track. Keep straight on for another half mile until you pass a lodge and through a gateway to emerge onto a road. 3/2 Turn right along the road (White Stubbs Lane) for one third of a mile. Soon after passing Bayford Kennels on your right, the road curves at a point where there is a bridleway on the left and a footpath on the right. Turn right there through a gate on a path which leads into Wormley Wood (owned by the Woodland Trust).

The path goes downhill and then down some steps across a stream then straight on uphill. Look for the arrows on the trees which waymark the route. The path goes down another dip, you cross another stream on a plank bridge and continue up the other side.

The path curves to the right and then to the left to continue in approximately a southward direction. It does another zig-zag right and left through a muddy area, goes more steeply downhill to cross a stream and then steeply up again on steps, and continues southwards through woods.

The path descends yet another dip, crosses a small stream on a plank bridge and goes up again. You reach an area which is more open where there is a ridge and a path going off to the left. Here you must go straight on along a narrower path between bushes. The path takes a somewhat zig-zag route, generally veering towards the left. You gradually get closer to a wood on your left. When you eventually reach the edge of the wood turn right along a better defined path. This path is just inside the wood with mature trees mainly to your left and to your right an area of saplings and general overgrowth. Keep straight on southwards along this path.

When you come to an apparent junction of paths fork slightly right. It is in effect almost straight on (southwards again). The main thing is not to stay on the wider track which turns left. You pass through a muddy area where there are old railway sleepers and continue straight on between bushes and small trees. At a minor junction fork left to stay on the main path. You reach a more open area where there is a junction of tracks and a barbed-wire fence on your right marking the boundary of a timber yard. Keeping the yard on your right, go through the open area to a gateway.

Go through the gate and continue along a gravel track. Pass under electricity wires. After a quarter of a mile, your track is joined by another from the right and there is a covered reservoir on your left. At the road go straight across onto Newgatestreet Road. Follow this road for one mile to return to the start of the walk.

Goff's Oak

9

WALK NO. 3

Bayford to Little Berkhamsted

Bayford – Tylers Causeway – Little Berkhamsted – Bayford

Distance 5½ miles

There is limited parking in the centre of this small village. Bayford Station is about half a mile away.

From the village take the road towards Brickendon. After passing the Baker Arms public house car park on your right, take a track that veers

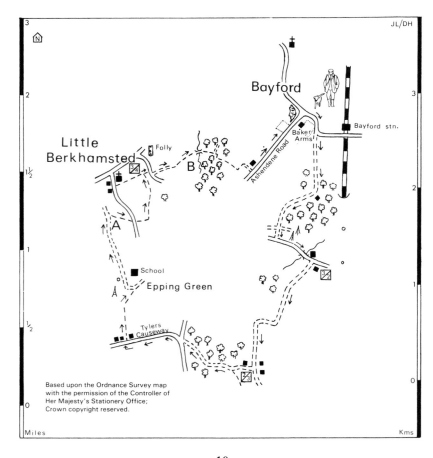

Based upon the Ordnance Survey map with the permission of the Controller of Her Majesty's Stationery Office; Crown copyright reserved.

to the right into Blackfan Wood where you soon pass under power lines at right angles. Follow this wide track which first leads you into the middle of the wood and then, just before a house, bends to the right and continues near the western edge of the wood. Ignoring another two wide tracks which branch off at right angles on your right you emerge from the wood opposite a garden centre and turn left along White Stubbs Lane.

When you pass a house called Old Claypits on the left, immediately turn right off the road, passing a gatehouse on the left. $\boxed{3/2}$ Continue along this wide tree-lined avenue which leads into Ponsbourne Park. Shortly before you come to a right-hand bend in the avenue, circular ventilation shafts from the Ponsbourne railway tunnel can be seen protruding in the fields on the left. Pass through a gate and continue past houses on the left built 1904–5. Just before the houses on the right turn right, $\boxed{2/3}$ along a track which slopes downhill and bears right through woodland. Keep to the main winding track and emerge from the estate by a gatehouse on the right, dated 1879. Here you cross the road and continue for half a mile along the road opposite (Tylers Causeway) which is signposted 'Essendon'. Ignore the first footpath on the right.

About 50 yards past a large bungalow called The Willows turn right onto a concealed footpath to Little Berkhamsted; it is just before the garage of Tylers Cottage. Proceed over a stile at the edge of a field to follow the boundary on the right and cross a second field via another stile. Then go over a further stile into a third field and, still with the boundary on the right, head towards radio masts and a water tower. After 170 yards turn right through the hedge (over a stile) and then immediately left with the boundary, which soon continues as a high brick wall, on your left.

Walk past the house on your left and through a gateway onto a lane. Turn left towards the radio mast and follow the lane, which turns right and passes Epping House School on your right and Woodcock Lodge on your left. Continue in the same direction along a wide gravel track until it turns right. Here you keep left on a wooded path which affords a good view to the west. This path brings you to a wooden gate (*see* sketch A). Pass through this gate and turn right. Cross the first field to a stile and follow the same line across a second field, ending up at a second stile. When you cross this you emerge directly onto a road which could be dangerous for children jumping down.

Carefully cross the road and continue through the gate opposite in the same general direction, with a hedge on the right. The path turns left with the field boundary to head towards the folly which is visible to the north. When you reach the corner of the field cross a stile on the right. Immediately turn left to continue towards the folly, passing through a short stretch of woodland. After two further fields with the boundary now on the right, you come to the field's northern boundary opposite a bungalow, where you turn right. $\boxed{3/4}$ After 20 yards cross a stile and turn right along the road (Bucks Alley) for 25 yards, then

11

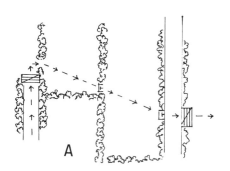

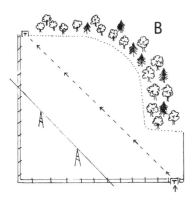

cross a stile on the left. Continue alongside Garden Cottage and then under the power lines in the first small field, keeping to the hedge on the right. When you cross into a larger field, follow a path nearly parallel to the power lines, to enter the wood by crossing a bridge near the corner of the field (*see* sketch B).

Continuing on the line of the bridge, follow the path through the woods, with barbed wire on your left. It turns right for a few paces and then continues left, in the same direction as before. Cross a drive at right angles and proceed as before, now with the wood on your right. You soon leave the wood by crossing a stile and maintain the same direction, with a hedge on your left. Then, turning to the left, still alongside the hedge, cross a stile. This leads to a track which turns right to join Ashendene Road alongside two semi-detached houses beside Bayford House. Turn left and follow the road for the last half mile back to the starting point in Bayford village.

The Five Horse Shoes, Little Berkhamsted — Whitwell 1892

WALK NO. 4

Little Berkhamsted to Letty Green

Little Berkhamsted – Water Hall – Letty Green – Little Berkhamsted

Distance 6 miles

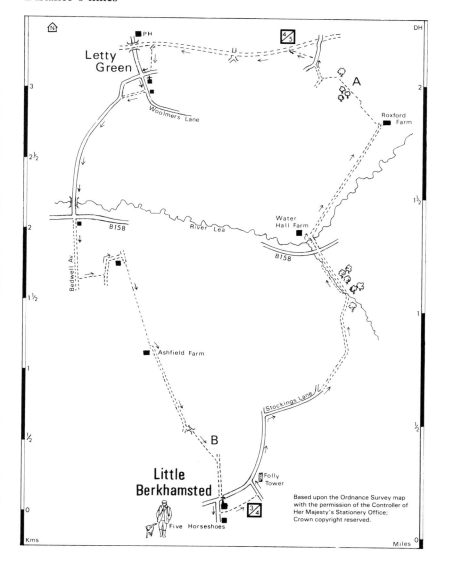

Parking is usually available outside the church or towards that end of the main road through the village.

Starting from the Five Horseshoes public house walk towards the church. Just before you reach it turn right over a stile. You are now in a grassy meadow with the church on your left. Keep straight on through the next field so that you have the hedge on your left until you reach a stile. $\boxed{3/4}$ Go over the stile onto the road with a brick wall opposite you, and turn left. Turn right at the road junction onto Robins Nest Hill. Use care on this road as there is no path on either side. Keep straight where there is a lodge on your right but look across to the gate on your left, where you have views across Hatfield and Welwyn Garden City.

After 400 yards turn right into Stockings Lane. This lane narrows and goes downhill. Where the lane bears left, leave it and go straight on along the stony track in front of you. There is a signpost 'Public Footpath to Bayford ³/₄'. The stony track goes gradually downhill, with a barbed-wire fence on your right and a hedge and trees on your left. To your front you can see woods. When you reach some buildings bear to your right, so that you pass the red brick house on your left. There is a signpost indicating 'Bridleway – Water Hall'. Go straight along a very narrow path going downhill with hedges on either side. The path becomes darker with hedges closing above and is generally muddy underfoot. This path takes you to a footbridge over a stream which is usually dried up.

At the bridge do not cross but immediately bear slightly left, uphill, away from the stream.* At the top of this bank, cross into a field where you bear right, so that you walk along the edge of the field with the open field to your left and the general wooded area to your right. Near the end of the field bear right, where there is a concrete bridge which you cross, and then immediately bear left.

You should now be on a track with hedges on either side. You pass some houses on your left to reach the B158 Lower Hatfield Road; be careful here. Cross the road and enter the premises of Water Hall, a gravel quarry. You are on a tarmac road. Pass under the electricity wires with a double pole on your right, cross the river and turn immediately right. After you pass the water authority concrete bridge the river bends away to the right but you keep straight on along a wide gravel track with a hedge on your right. The gravel operators may well have made some tracks to the left, but you must ignore them. Turn left when you reach the corner of the field near the buildings of Roxford Farm. Do not turn right where you see a white gate on your right-hand side, but continue straight up the field-edge track towards Grotto Wood. There

*There is an alternative permissive route along the far bank of the stream which is OK except when the stream is in flood. Cross the footbridge and turn left along the bank. Follow the stream until you emerge onto the hedged track just before the houses.

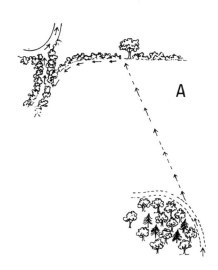

A

is a signpost and you follow the direction of the arm which says 'Footpath – East End Green'. You are now going uphill with the hedge on your right and the field to your left. When you reach the corner of the field it is worth looking at the view behind you.

Turn right and immediately left to continue in approximately the same direction as before. You are now going gradually uphill, with the wood on your left and the field on your right. You come to the point where the wood on your left curves away. At the very start of that curve keep on going straight ahead into the field and leaving the edge of the wood (*see* sketch A). Walk straight across this large field, where the right of way is often not visible, aiming for a large solitary tree on the far side.

When you reach the tree, turn left along the edge of the field, with the hedge on your right. In 120 yards find a small gap in the hedge on your right. Turn right through the gap, go down three steps and bear right, on a track, until you emerge onto a bend in a tarmac lane. Turn right and in about 40 yards turn left off the lane at a gateway. Walk down a slight hill keeping the hedge and ditch about 8 yards distance on your right. Pass close to a power pole, bearing very slightly right to the corner of the field, and cross the ditch into the next field.

Continue in the same direction slightly downhill passing a large tree on your right. At the bottom of the field cross the plank bridge. Wild watercress grows here. Twenty yards ahead you see steps to a disused railway track. This is the line of the former Hertford and Welwyn Junction Railway which has been converted by the County Council into a route for walkers, riders and cyclists. It is also a link in the Lea Valley Walk (see note on page 17).

Climb the steps and turn left to go along the course of the old

15

railway. 4/5 Follow the railway track for a little over a half mile. This means you keep straight on where the first footpath crosses until you come to a stretch where there is wooden fencing and a picnic area on your right on the platform of what was once Cole Green Station. Look for a concrete ladder stile on your left, opposite a gate on your right. Turn left there, going over the ladder stile.

Proceed along this very narrow path until you reach a road. Turn right. At the road junction, by the church, turn left along Woolmers Lane. About 240 yards along the road, opposite house number 25, turn right along a track. Follow the track, which has a small woodland on the left for 300 yards. When you reach the road turn left.

In just over a half a mile the road goes over the River Lea and soon after that you come to a junction of roads where you cross the B158. Go straight on through the gates along Bedwell Avenue. Pass Hertford Lodge on your left on a wide bridleway. In a quarter of a mile, 100 yards before a tall conifer hedge, look carefully for a left turn which leads up to a gate and a stile. When you have crossed the stile go uphill, across a large field, aiming for a big oak tree you can see on the horizon. Go over the gate by the big tree and turn left onto a gravel road passing a large white house on your left.

When you reach a small white bungalow, turn right onto a footpath signposted to Little Berkhamsted. In about 50 yards cross a stile and then proceed into a field where you have a hedge on your right and the field on your left. At the corner of the field cross the stile to enter another large field which you have to cross, maintaining the same direction. If the right of way is not visible, aim for a point well to the left of a white bungalow you see beyond the field boundary. As you cross the field you pass under electricity cables and gradually converge with the hedge on your left. Eventually the path runs alongside the hedge and you continue to the corner of the field where you cross a stile. In the next field continue in the same direction with a barbed-wire fence on your left. On reaching the corner of the field, cross the stile. You will probably notice the smell of the pig farm. Almost directly in front of you is a very muddy bridleway with hedges on each side.

Continue on this bridleway which means you maintain the same general direction. Keep straight on where a path joins on your left. After a quarter of a mile you cross a concrete bridge with wooden fencing and then fork left to emerge into a large field. Sometimes the right of way here is not visible. You bear slightly left to cross the field diagonally, aiming for a gap in the left-hand hedge this side of the distant opposite corner (*see* sketch B). You start on level ground and then go gradually uphill. There is a copse which you pass about 200 yards to your right and you gradually converge with the hedge on your left. Aim for the first gateway and pass through onto a track where you bear right. (There are good views behind you on a clear day.) The track brings you to a road where you turn right. In a few yards turn left at the war memorial to reach the Five Horseshoes public house.

B
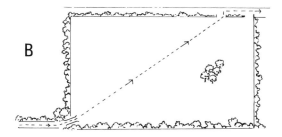

The Lea Valley Walk is a fifty mile regional route from the Thames to the source of the Lea at Luton. Over the last twenty years, many people and organisations have worked towards the production of a co-ordinated route through the London Boroughs, The Lea Valley Regional Park, Hertfordshire and Bedfordshire. The route follows tow-paths, field paths, former railway tracks and park paths mainly by connecting public rights of way.

The Lea Valley Walk is waymarked and signposted. For ease of navigation follow the **SWAN** symbol. There are local links and connecting routes into the rest of the rights of way network.

For more information, contact:
Countryside Management Service
Planning & Environment Dept
County Hall
HERTFORD
SG13 8DN

Hertingfordbury to Marden Hill

Hertingfordbury – Birch Green – Marden Hill (near Tewin) – Hertingfordbury

Distance 6½ miles

Parking is easiest at the north end of the village on the cul-de-sac piece of the old road near the A414 roundabout. There is also space to park in St Mary's Lane near the church.

This walk starts from St Mary's Church, Hertingfordbury. Many of the paths used on this walk will be affected by new gravel pits. When these changes are made the East Herts Footpath Society will endeavour to get the diverted routes properly waymarked.

Walk south along the lane so that you leave St Mary's Church on your left-hand side. Pass under the bridge of the disused railway and turn left and immediately left again, climbing the bank on to the old railway. Turn left again, so that you are now on top of the bridge crossing the road and heading in a westerly direction along the route of the old railway. After about three-quarters of a mile deviate slightly

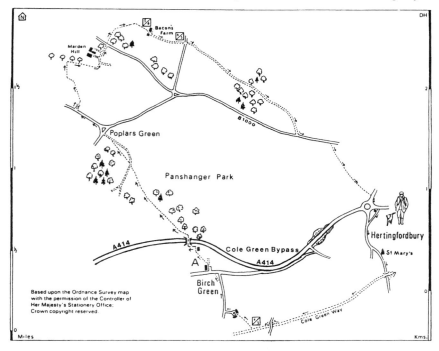

to the right up an embankment, where you cross a lane (which leads to Staines Green), and down the embankment on the other side of the lane to rejoin the railway track. Continue for about 200 yards keeping a sharp lookout for a point where another path crosses; this is indicated by flights of steps on both sides of the track. $\boxed{4/5}$ Turn right, go down the steps, over a stile and across an open field towards some distant houses. When you reach the far side of the field, cross a stile between the gardens and then a short tunnel takes you under the upper floors of the houses. When you emerge into a cul-de-sac continue straight ahead and when you reach the road junction turn right. You are now at Birch Green.

It is best to use the footpath on the left side of the green to avoid walking in the roadway as you near the main road. Bear left across the green, passing the war memorial just to your right. When you reach the main road cross over and turn left, and walk about 50 yards along the pavement to a signpost marked 'Public Footpath – Poplars Green' beside a house. Turn right up a track which passes houses on your left. Just after the last house you reach the drive to Beechleight Farm. Go partway up the drive looking for a stile in a fence over to your left. When you reach a point on the drive where the stile is lined up with the far corner of the field (*see* sketch A), leave the driveway and proceed over the stile straight towards the far corner.

At the corner of the field, cross a stile, pass between bushes and immediately swing round to the right. Pass through a gap to continue a few yards between bushes. When you emerge, walk towards the bypass, keeping the garden hedge to your right. Cross the footbridge over the bypass. Follow the edge of the woodland, which takes a zig–zag course, keeping the woods to your right. Eventually you will reach a part which is more open.

Bear right to cross the open area, where there is normally a grassy path between ferns. You will be going slightly downhill. (This part of the path, Hertingfordbury No. 10, may be diverted when more of Panshanger Park is opened up for gravel extraction.) Keeping the fence to your right, the path bears left down the hill.

Cross a substantial stile and go straight on across the open field. Keep straight on where you have the boundary fence of a wood on your left to reach another stile. Cross that and bear slightly right to join a gravel track. Look up to the overhead power line and bear left, leaving the track to follow the route of the cables. The path passes between some bushes and then across an open area. Where the power lines cease, keep straight on until you emerge onto a lane near the lodge. This is Poplars Green.

Cross the lane and keep straight on up a short section of road to the main road junction, signposted 'Welwyn B1000'. Cross over the B1000 carefully and turn left, walking along the road in the direction of Welwyn for 250 yards until you reach a stile by the side of a gate on

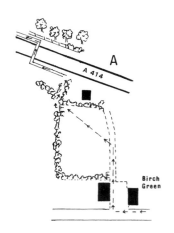

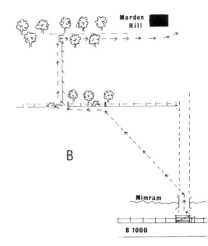

your right. Climb over the stile and in a few yards you cross a bridge over the river Mimram and keep straight on. You reach another stile, which you cross, then turn half left, and continue diagonally across an open field, going gradually uphill. Looking to your left you will see farm buildings and, beyond them on the skyline, tall buildings in Welwyn Garden City (*see* sketch B).

When you reach the far side of the field turn left and follow the line of trees on your right. Look for a gap in the barbed-wire fence on your right and turn right there. Do not go over the piece of wooden fence in front of you but immediately bear left, through the bushes, and emerge into a field with a wire fence on your right. Cross the field and, keeping the fence on your right, aim for a line of tall trees. (This path, Tewin No. 22, may be diverted when the land is opened up for gravel extraction.) When you reach the avenue of trees, turn sharp right, cross a stile and proceed along the avenue. Keep straight on where the avenue ends and pass in front of the big house, Marden Hill. Keep straight on, with railings on your left. When you reach the corner of the railings, turn left so that you continue with the railings on your left. You soon reach a gate and stile. Cross the stile and follow the track ahead of you, cross the drive that leads to Marden Hill on your left and keep straight on. You have railings to your left, with buildings beyond and a fence and field on your right. Pass the entrance to Marden Cottage and woodland on your left and emerge onto a road. Cross the road to a farm track.

Follow this track with an open field on your left and a wood (Red Wood) on your right. Keep to this track close to the edge of the field as it curves right. You continue along a stretch which has a hedge on the right and the field on the left until you reach a stile. Cross the stile

20

and turn half right, aiming for a metal gate and then the stile and gate you can see on the far side of the field. Cross this stile and turn a little to your left to go along a track between farm buildings at Bacon's Farm. $\boxed{5/6}$ Continue on a good gravel track between hedges. Keep straight on across a tarmac road onto a bridleway. $\boxed{6/5}$ The track remains fairly well-defined on the ground but as you get nearer to the woods it becomes narrower. Close to the woods there is a section where you have woodland on your right and the field on your left and soon after that you enter the woods.

Going through the wood try to maintain the same general direction, ignoring the tracks to the right. You pass through an area where the woods are thick on both sides but after that there is a section where you are close to the boundary of the wood on your left. Keep close to the left-hand boundary and when you reach the end of the wood keep straight on along a path where there is a hedge on your left and an open field on your right.

When you reach the point where there is a small woodland in front of you, keep on the gravel track which turns right and goes downhill. You then go up a gradient and when you reach the road turn left and walk along the grass verge for about 400 yards. Just before you reach the built-up area you will see a gateway on the right side of the road. Cross the road and enter the field; the path crosses the field diagonally to the left towards the woodland. (This path may be diverted when the area is opened up for gravel extraction.) When you reach the far side of the field, enter the wood and then continue in the same direction. Ignore a track on your left which leads deeper into the wood and keep on until you emerge into an open area.

Follow a fence on your right with the wood further away to your left. The boundary of the wood gradually converges again with the line of the path and there you continue with the edge of the wood close to your left. At the junction of tracks turn right along a piece of track, usually muddy, with fences on both sides. Look carefully for the place where the path turns diagonally left away from the track and turn left there. Do not go straight ahead downhill where there is a notice 'Private Estate – Keep Out'. Continue with woods on your right and the fence on your left. The path continues through the woods, going gradually downhill, and emerges onto a road. Cross carefully and turn right to the roundabout. Cross over the main road at a convenient point to the left of the roundabout and take the side road back to Hertingfordbury and St Mary's Church.

WALK NO. 6

Bramfield Woods going South

Bramfield Woods – Queen Hoo Hall – Bramfield Village – Bramfield Woods

Distance 4½ miles

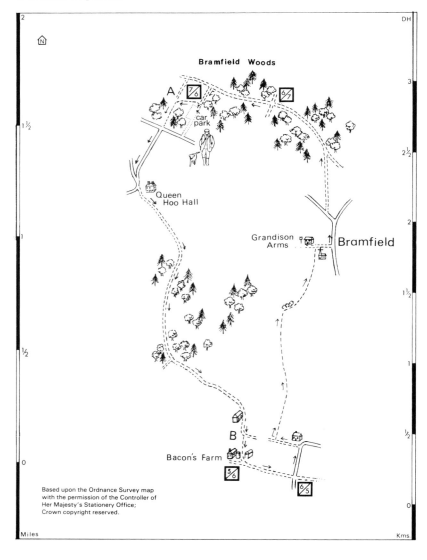

Based upon the Ordnance Survey map with the permission of the Controller of Her Majesty's Stationery Office; Crown copyright reserved.

Easiest parking is in the Forestry Commission car park which is just off the north-eastern side of the Datchworth road, 1 mile from Bramfield (GR 283167). (This is the same starting point as walk No. 7 – Bramfield going North.) An alternative starting point is outside the Grandison Arms public house in Bramfield village.

Walk north away from the road out of the car park through a wooden barrier by a Forestry Commission sign. 7/6 Turn left and follow a path marked by red-topped posts through the woods. Ten yards after a right turn, turn left off the waymarked path (*see* sketch A) onto a path going downhill. Cross a small ditch at a dip in the path, at the fork after the ditch bear left and in about 30 yards you will emerge on to a gravel track. There turn left going downhill. When you reach the road, cross it, and continue along Tewin Hill, the lane signposted 'Queen Hoo Tewin'. Keep straight on where Queen Hoo Lane joins on your right.

At the bend in the lane walk straight on, along a track signposted 'Public Bridleway to Tewin 1'. (To your left is Queen Hoo Hall.) This is a gravel track between fences and bushes. On reaching an open field, maintain the same general direction going downhill along the track. There are open fields on both sides and a good view ahead. The track veers slightly to the right but maintains the same general direction. The ground levels out as you get closer to Bramfield Park Wood ahead of you and the track bears a little to the right just before it enters the woods.

Keep straight on at a very muddy section where another track crosses and you will see a Forestry Commission sign on your left. Ignore this sign and keep straight ahead through the wood where it can still be extremely muddy. Where the path appears to fork towards open fields by a rustic fence covered in bushes, bear left and then right, so that you are just inside the wood. This section is very muddy indeed and you may find firmer routes through the bushes on either side. Through the bushes to your right you should see an open field. Eventually you start going uphill again on a muddy section with woods on both sides.

Before the wood on your right ends a path joins on your right, but you should walk ahead to the left, slightly outside the wood, with the field to your right and the wood to your left (*see* sketch B). About 100 yards beyond the wood boundary you fork right across an open field. The track is usually visible. There are good views here.

Looking across the field you can see the brown building of Westend Farm with a long roof. Aim just to the left of the buildings. You are now going gradually downhill, with a large field on both sides. Nearer to the buildings a hedge and ditch on your left gradually converge with the path. At the old buildings turn slightly right, to pass them on your right.

Ignoring the bridleway going off left, you soon come to a junction

A

where a track joins from the right. There you turn left and almost immediately turn right to stay on the track. You have open fields on both sides. Soon the track turns left and there you leave it to go straight on (*see* sketch B).

You pass through a small group of young trees to find a gap in the hedge ahead. Go through the gap and straight on across the field. You see Bacons Farm ahead to your right. Aim for the big tree straight ahead and eventually pass it on your right with the grounds of the farmhouse beyond to your right and a field on your left. You pass between farm buildings to reach another track where you turn left.
5/6 You then pass under electricity wires keeping a power pole to your left. This gravel track soon has banks and bushes on both sides. Where the gravel track crosses a lane turn left along this lane. 6/5 You pass under electricity wires with a power pole to your left. Just before the sharp right bend in the lane, turn left in front of Westend House.

You are now on a gravel track with bushes on both sides. You pass under electricity wires and soon afterwards reach a point where the track takes a slight bend to the right and then to the left. Just as it takes the bend to the left you will see a double power pole to your

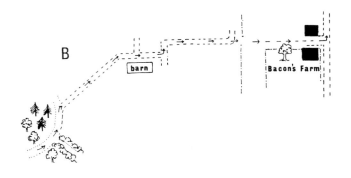

B

barn

Bacon's Farm

right. Turn right and aim straight for the double pole and you may notice the remains of a hedge and ditch on your right as you proceed. Pass close to the double pole on your right and follow the line of the overhead wires straight ahead of you.

Continue straight on where a track crosses just before a power pole. At the sixth pole, which has double insulators, the wires fork further to the right but here you must keep straight on for just over 150 yards. The wires are now further away to your right. Turn right and keep a short section of hedge on your left as you proceed. About 70 yards brings you to a power pole, where you are once again under the wires and there turn left. You go downhill with open fields on both sides, keeping the wires a little to your left. Ahead you may see the spire of Bramfield Church through the trees.

At the bottom of the dip cross a stile after an earth bridge a little to the right and then continue uphill. Aim towards a stile by a large tree which appears to the right of the church spire. Pass the big tree to your right and continue straight, entering a sports field.

Continue along the right-hand edge of the sports field and you pass a kissing-gate on your right, which is the entrance to Bramfield churchyard. (If you wish you can turn right there and then turn left at the main road on the far side.) Continuing straight on along the edge of the sports field, you pass some swings on your left and you see the Grandison Arms public house ahead. At the road turn right, and at the next road junction turn left along the main road. Keep straight on along the main road and continue on at the road junction where the main road bears very slightly left, signposted 'Datchworth 2½ miles'.

About 140 yards after the road junction fork right, going off the road, following a 'Public Bridleway' sign. You go gradually uphill on a muddy track. There are bushes on both sides. You pass under electricity wires close to a pole on your right. A very muddy section here. Continue on the track uphill. You may find drier routes on the right-hand bank, but keep away from the edge of an old chalk pit. Keep straight on at the gap in the fence. The path continues uphill into Bramfield Woods.

Keep on the main path ignoring minor paths going off to the right. The path (marked by red-topped posts) levels out and veers to the left. Keep straight on down into a dip where another path joins on your right. Go uphill to reach a gravel track and proceed straight across this. 6/7 You are now on a very wide grassy path. You come to a very muddy section and the path veers marginally to the right. You eventually reach a gravel track and there turn left. Keep straight on where a track joins on your left and continue on to the car park where you started the walk.

WALK NO. 7

Bramfield Woods going North

Bramfield Woods – Perrywood Farm – Watton-at-Stone – Great Gobions Farm – Bramfield Woods

Distance 4¹/₂ miles

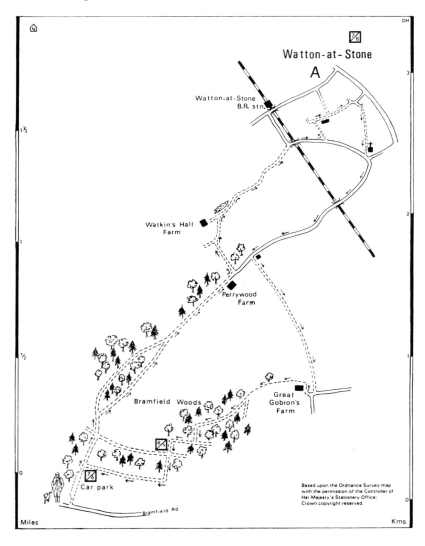

Easiest parking is in the Forestry Commission car park which is just off the north-eastern side of the Datchworth road, one mile from Bramfield (GR 283167). (This is the same starting point as Walk No. 6 – Bramfield going South.) An alternative starting point is the station car park in Watton-at-Stone.

Walk away from the road through the wooden barrier where there is a Forestry Commission sign. 7/6 Continue on a wide gravel track with woods on your left. Keep straight on where a track joins on your right and again when you cross a wide track.

When you reach a junction of tracks at a neck of the woods between open fields take the right fork along the edge of the wood (Long Walk, Perrywood Lane), so that you have the wood on your left and a field on your right. There is a good view from here. Keep on the downhill track with woods on your left, passing a path to your left, and eventually on your left you pass a Forestry Commission sign. Soon after that you reach a section of the track which has fields on each side. Continue straight on where you have hedgerows on each side and you will see the farm buildings of Perrywood Farm.

Pass through the farm with buildings on your right and a few yards after that turn left along a bridleway. The bridleway starts off as a muddy track between bushes and then becomes a gravel track with open fields on each side. At a T-junction of tracks, turn right and immediately pass through an iron gate, keeping on the gravel track so that you pass the buildings of Watkins Hall Farm on your left. At the junction of tracks opposite Watkins Hall turn right along a surfaced lane towards a wood. You should see two ponds, one just before the right turn and one soon after. Both will be on your left. Pass through a gateway with a cattle grid and keep straight on along a lane, passing Watkins Cottage on your right.

At the junction of lanes keep straight on, crossing the bridge over the railway. When the lane reaches a wooded area turn left, along a path which has a chainlink fence on the left and a hedge on the right. The hedge is the boundary of a school playing-field. At the T-junction of paths turn right so that you still have the school on your right. When you reach the roadway (Rectory Lane) turn right, and in a few yards turn left, along a surfaced path (School Lane) which has hedges on each side. Where a path joins on the left, keep to the right. 7/8*

You reach a part where there is a playing field and sports pavilion on your right and a low brick wall runs alongside the path. At the point where there are swings on the right, turn right along a narrower path, so keeping the swings to your right and houses on your left. (If you wish to get to the main road in Watton-at-Stone do not make the right turn by the swings, but keep straight along the wide path.)

*There is no actual link point with Walk No. 8 which passes a short distance away (see sketch A).

The narrow path brings you to the church, where the path chicanes, keeping outside the churchyard, and soon brings you to a lane where you turn left. The lane goes downhill for a short distance with the church on your left to a junction where you turn right up Perrywood Lane. You are now going uphill directly away from the church towards Watton Green. Carry straight on where a path joins on your left. Continue along this lane going downhill, crossing over the railway. Keep going for another quarter mile downhill and then uphill until you pass a point where a path joins on your right and soon after that you pass on your left the first house after the railway bridge.

At this point, you turn left along a bridleway. You keep straight on along this bridleway, which has open fields and good views to the left, for about two-thirds of a mile. When you reach a metalled road turn right. Very soon, where the road does a left bend, bear right to pass through Great Gobions Farm. You pass close to the farmhouse on your right, keeping the barns on your left. When you reach the field beyond the farm buildings turn left, so that you continue with the field on your right and new barns on your left. After you reach the end of the farm buildings continue with a ditch on your right along the edge of the field until you reach the corner of the wood. Continue in the same direction, with the trees on your right.

About a hundred yards from the corner you bear right between two oak trees to enter the wood. Soon after entering the wood you meet a junction of tracks. Take the right fork which has a wooden barrier and stile across it. Ignore tracks to left and right. About 300 yards beyond the barrier, where the track makes a left bend, follow it and then turn right at the T-junction of tracks.

You should now be on a track with a firm gravel surface. After 200 yards bear left to continue along the gravel surface. Keep straight on where a wide grass track crosses. 6/7 Where the gravel track makes a right turn follow it, and at this point you should see beyond the woods open countryside to your left. Stay on the gravel track until you reach a T-junction and there turn left to return to the car park.

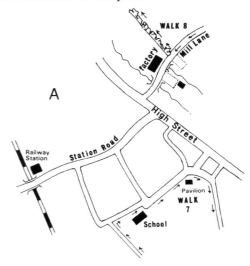

WALK NO. 8

Watton-at-Stone going North

Watton-at-Stone – Burn's Green – Hebing End – Gregory's Farm – Watton-at-Stone

Distance 7 miles

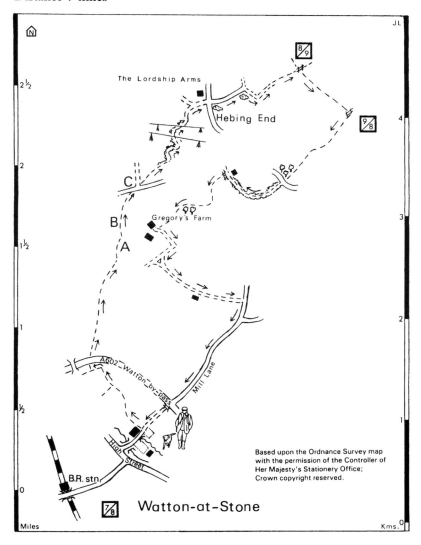

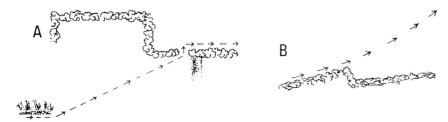

There are several roads in the village where cars can be left. Mill Lane at GR 301195 is a cul-de-sac where there is usually room to park.

Watton-at-Stone lies between Hertford and Stevenage a little to the west of the new bypass on the A602; it can also be reached by rail. An alternative starting point is from the Lordship Arms public house at Hebing End.

The description begins at Mill Lane, which lies on the east side of Watton High Street, a little north of where Station Road joins on the opposite side of the street. ⬚7/8*⬚ Cross the bridge over the stream and just past the factory on your left you turn left onto a bridleway and continue along the edge of the field with the hedge on your left and the field on your right. Where the hedge ends and a track joins on your left continue on, bearing slightly to the right. You pass close to a pair of large trees to your left and as you near the Watton bypass you reach another hedgerow. Turn left, alongside the road on a path between hedges, and continue 50 yards downhill. A few yards before the bottom of the dip, at a point where there is a small ditch or stream, turn right and emerge onto the bypass (A602).

Cross over the road with care, into the field directly opposite, following the line of the ditch, with trees and a hedge to your left and the open field on your right. Continue with the ditch on your left for a little more than a quarter mile, then keep straight on where a concrete farm track crosses. Later, you come to a junction with another path on your left by an earth bridge; ignore this and go ahead until you reach a point where the ditch on your left ends. Here bear slightly left and cross the open field (*see* sketch A). You gradually converge with a hedge on your left, at a point where a short ridge runs at right angles to the hedge. Here turn left through the gap in the hedge up a bank.

Immediately after passing through the hedge and ascending into the next field turn right, so that you continue with the hedge on your right,

*See sketch A at end of preceding walk.

30

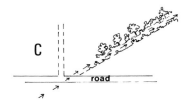

following the curve of the hedge for about 140 yards to where the hedge kinks to the right (*see* sketch B). This is a large field and you are in the lowest part of a small dip. The field rises a little to your left and there is a small hill to your right. On the distant horizon you will see some woods. From the bottom of the dip, strike away from the hedge, ascending the valley floor towards the lowest point on the near horizon in front of the woods.

As you cross the field you come to a small bank. On the road over to your left, you may see a new signpost. Do not turn towards it but continue across the bank in the original direction.

You should emerge onto a road by a bridge where a farm track joins on the other side. Do not take this track, which leaves the road at right angles, but use the less obvious path, proceeding in almost the same direction you were travelling in across the previous field (*see* sketch C). At first you follow the right side of a ditch towards a wood on the right, then along a narrow path between hedges. Gradually the path improves and becomes a firm wide path. There is a section which is always wet because of drainage from adjoining fields. Pass a pond on your left and bear right where the path curves, continuing through a muddy section and passing under two sets of overhead wires before emerging onto a lane. Bear right along the lane, continue past the houses and you will arrive at a road junction beside the Lordship Arms.

Cross over the road and walk straight down the lane opposite, which is signposted 'Hebing End'. At the far end of the tarred road is a pond on your right and just beyond that a bridleway. Turn right along this bridleway, walking with a barbed-wire fence on your left and a garden on your right. Bear left, following the track, and continue with a barbed-wire fence to your left. You go gradually downhill and at the point where the track takes a right-hand bend you keep straight on, down the hill, with trees and a hedge on your left.

Near the bottom of the hill you pass through the hedge on your left, then continue in the same direction as before, with the hedge now on your right. Ten yards before you reach a wooden bridge over a stream you will find a bridle gate on your right. 8/9 Turn right through this gate into an arable field. Follow the wire fence on your left to the next corner and turn left into a meadow over a small bridge. Then turn right and make for an iron gate in the corner to your left.

9/8

At the corner, do not leave the field but turn right and follow the fence on your left next to a deep ditch. This is The Old Bourne, which joins the River Beane near Watton-at-Stone. You re-cross the ditch which you crossed on entering this meadow and continue by the fence for about 250 yards to the next corner.

At this corner, turn left onto a track and immediately turn right, so that you continue in the next field with the hedge on your left. Keep close to this hedge, which makes a number of turns, and at the corner of the field pass through the intersecting hedge and continue uphill in the same direction as before, again with a hedge on your left.

After about 350 yards the track goes into a hollow lane between some bushes, and gradually uphill through a wooded area, following the same general direction, until it emerges onto a road.

Cross the road to another track which becomes very muddy. After 250 yards, you pass a pond on the left and the track turns right. There are arable fields to the left and paddocks to the right. Continue until you reach a thatched cottage on your right, 40 yards short of the road. If you stand with your back to the cottage you will be facing a gateway and stile into a field where there are usually ponies. Cross the stile into the field. The path runs roughly parallel to the hedge on your left. Cross another stile and continue on the same line.

The path converges with the hedge on your left and you cross several more stiles while following a line of telegraph poles in the hedge. You enter a field where there is a wood on your left and a clump of bushes surrounding a pond on your right.

As you leave this field, you pass under the telephone line and turn left for a few yards before turning right to continue to follow the edge of the wood. Where the telephone line leaves the wood, you pass under it again to a corner where there is an overgrown gate leading into a narrow grass field. Cross into this field and continue in the same direction, passing a pond to your left, to a field gate. You then cross a garden to an unmade road close to Gregory's Farm.

Turn left along this road, which is fenced on both sides, and follow it when it turns right, keeping a hedge to your left. At the junction of tracks where there is a power pole, fork left, and continue down the road following the route of some power lines. There are open fields on each side and to your right is a view across to Watton and Bramfield Woods. Further along the road you pass a triangulation point and communications relay on your left and farm buildings on your right. Eventually the farm road swings right and joins a public road. Turn right down this lane which is joined in 100 yards by another lane from the left. Continue straight on downhill until you reach a major road. This is the Watton bypass. Cross over taking great care of the fast traffic, go through the gate opposite, and continue down the disused lane in the same direction as before and you will shortly arrive at your starting point in Watton-at-Stone.

Watton Church — Buckler 1832

WALK NO. 9

Green End to Haultwick

Green End – Haultwick – Green End

Distance 5½ miles

There is usually room to park at the side of the fairly wide lane that runs from the church up to Green End (GR 331224).

This walk starts about half a mile from Little Munden Church on the road that leads from Dane End to Green End.

Follow the road round its left-hand turn and then keep straight on,

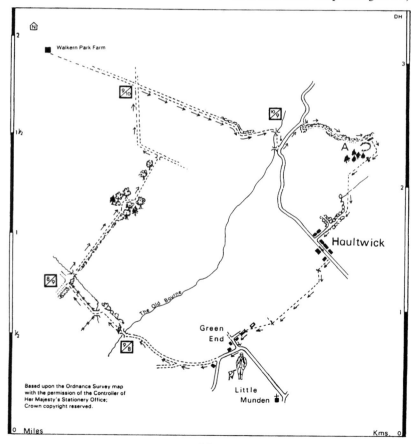

ignoring a lane on your right. After about 150 yards you pass a pond on your right; wild irises grow here. At the point where the road takes a left turn, where there is a house on the corner, go straight on along the track to the right of the house (Peartree Cottage). After 250 yards, you come to a fork where there is a power pole bearing a transformer on your right. Take the lesser track forking right. This track goes gradually downhill and at the lowest point there is a river bed usually dried-up. Cross the concrete bridge, $\boxed{9/8}$ go through an iron gate on your left and then immediately turn right, so that you now continue in a long wide meadow, in roughly the same direction as you were travelling previously. Usually there are cattle in this meadow and it is important to latch the gate. Part way along you will find that the meadow narrows and that there is a wire fence to your left. Where this fence starts, bear left over a small bridge and then right through the fence to continue in your original direction with the wire fence on your right. At the right-hand corner of the field, you go through a gateway in the hedge $\boxed{8/9}$ and turn right over a wooden bridge.

After crossing the bridge go straight up the hill in front of you, so that you have bushes and woods on your right and the field on your left. When you reach the top of the hill there are good views to your left. You reach a corner of the field where there are woods in front of you. Follow the path to the left as it zig-zags through the wood for just over 100 yards. Turn right when you emerge from the wood and follow it for a few yards to a point where the woodland bends. Here you bear to the left away from the wood and walk towards a line of trees which begins about 100 yards out in the field. These mark the position of a hedge. Keep the hedge on your left and the field on your right. Where the hedge on your left ceases, cross an earth bridge over a ditch onto a track and turn left. After 130 yards turn right with the track, so that you continue with a ditch and a hedge on your left and the open field on your right.

After another 500 yards you come to a T-junction with a stony track where you turn right $\boxed{9/10}$ to go downhill beside a ditch.

Turn right where the hedge turns right and then, in about 60 yards turn left. You are descending to the valley of the Old Bourne. $\boxed{10/9}$ When you reach the bottom, turn right and then, a little further on, cross the Old Bourne onto a grassy track. Keep on this track until you reach the road, where you turn left.

The road goes up a fairly steep hill. Go past one path on the right-hand side before you reach the top of the hill. Take the next path to the right, which is just before the top of the hill. (The third path on the right is the driveway to Stag Hall Farm. If you are still on the road at this point then you will have to turn back about 40 yards.) The track you require doubles back above the road for about 50 yards and then turns left to follow a path which has bushes on either side. This path is a long steady uphill climb.

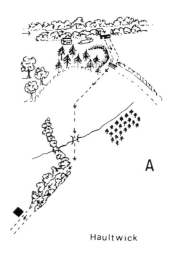

A

Haultwick

You reach a part where there are tall trees, a pond and then some farm buildings on your right. Nearby is a second pond and a wooden gate with a cattle grid on your right. Turn right through the gate. The field on your left is usually a green meadow and on your right there is a moat (*see* sketch A). Continue along the track, which bears right when you reach another gate with a stile alongside it.

There is a small plantation of trees on your right, and where these end you enter an open field, where it is often difficult to see the line of the path across the field. You will find that you are about 200 yards from some woods ahead and to your right. To the left there is a small plantation of fir trees and beyond that a ditch. The line of the path continues into the field in the same direction that you have been travelling along the track and then bends to the left (*see* sketch A). Cross the ditch which divides the field by a small earth bridge about 100 yards beyond the plantation and aim for the left end of the hedge on the far side of the field.

When you reach the hedge, follow it on your right around the corner. After about 40 yards the hedge thickens, and it is in fact the border of a green lane with a double hedge. Choose the first opportunity to get into the green lane and continue in the same direction. When you come to a junction of green lanes, bear left uphill. Continue on this green lane for another 100 yards until you emerge onto a road in the village of Haultwick (pronounced 'Artic' in the local dialect).

At the T-junction turn left, towards the centre of Haultwick, keeping a lookout on the right-hand side in about 150 yards for the footpath along the edge of the garden of a new house called Haultwick Farm, just past a bungalow called The Cranny. Turn right there so that you walk along with a hedge on your right. You cross a stile into a field

36

behind the houses (which may be sub-divided into smaller enclosures by wire fences) and continue in the same direction to a stile in the hedgerow about 200 yards from the road behind you.

In the next field turn approximately half left. You will see a tree and, just to the right of it, a stile; make straight for that stile across the corner of the field. Cross the stile and turn right, so that you walk along with the hedge on your right and the field on your left. At the corner of the field there is another stile. Cross this and continue in the next field again with the hedge on your right and the field on your left. Go straight on through more fields (the number varies as fences are put up or taken down) until you approach some tall trees. There you cross a stile so that you now have the hedge on your left and you veer slightly to the right. You pass a pond or very marshy area on your right and you aim straight for the houses which you can see about 300 yards in front, beyond a sports field.

Walking across the sports field you pass the pavilion on your right. In the far right-hand corner of the field you pass through a gateway which leads to a gravel lane between houses in Green End. When you reach the street turn left. Very soon you come to a T-junction where you turn left again and you should recognise this as the lane on which you started the walk.

WALK NO. 10

Moor Green

Moor Green – Back Lane – Wood End – Sander's Green – Parker's Green – Muncher's Green – Moor Green

Distance 5 miles

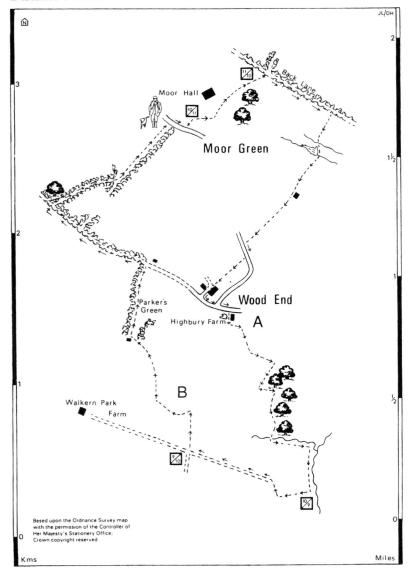

Moor Green is a hamlet halfway between Wood End and Ardeley which, sadly, no longer possesses its own pub. There is space to park off the road where it runs through the Green at GR 323267.

Coming from Wood End the first house in Moor Green is The Goose, which used to be a public house until about 1980. Start from the middle of the Green walking south-east back along the road towards Wood End. Before you get to The Goose look for the gravel track on the left, where there is a 'Public Footpath' sign. Turn left along this track towards the low farm buildings of Moor Hall (a large brick house). As you go along the track you will see a white house and a small white bungalow across the green to your right. 10/11

Approach Moor Hall, go through an old gateway and turn right over a stile, continuing with a hedge on your right. You pass close to a power pole on your right and go under electricity wires. Look for a wooden stile in the hedge on your right. Cross this stile and then turn left. As the hedge on your left curves away keep straight on, so that you cross the field diagonally, keeping to the left of a lone tree in the middle of the field.

You gradually move away from the power line that you can see on your left as you get nearer to the wood on your right. You converge with a hedge on your left and in this you will see the wide gap of an old gateway. Go through it and then bear slightly right. Keep on a straight line which takes you to the corner of the wood and continue walking around the edge of the woodland for about 90 yards. To your left, about 150 yards away, you will see a bridle gate and stile in the hedgerow. Veer away to the left to cross the field, passing under electricity wires, towards the gate and stile. Cross the stile and turn right along the Roman road 'Back Lane'. 11/10

Walk along Back Lane for about 500 yards, keeping a lookout through the hedge on your right for a point where there is a hedgerow going at right angles across a large field. At this point in Back Lane you should see a wooden post, on the left of the path, with blue and yellow arrows. Turn right into the open field. With the hedge on your left and the field on your right you immediately pass close to a power pole with wires going in three directions. Near the next corner of the field turn left, and about 15 yards later turn right, across a stile in a barbed-wire fence.

Veer left, then cross a muddy area, where there is a low wall and water to your right. Go on uphill through a small wooded area, keeping fairly close to the boundary on your right.

Aim towards a brick building and close to it there is a barbed-wire fence. Cross the stile in the fence into an overgrown garden just to the right of the building and continue with a hedge a few yards to your right. At the top of the field, you pass a lone tree and reach a deep ditch.

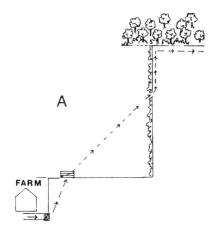

A

Cross the ditch and pass through a gap in the far side hedge. You now have to maintain the same general direction across the large field you have entered.

Cross the field towards a house and a wooden barn on the far side. Just over halfway across the field turn slightly to the right towards a gateway and a footpath sign at the corner of the field where the path joins the road.

Turn left at the road. About 80 yards further on turn right, just before the 'Wood End' sign. There are two field entrances. Go through the one on the left, where there should be a footpath signpost and cross the field diagonally. There are two power poles in the field and you aim for the furthermost one, which is at the end of a hedgerow. Pass close to that power pole and then follow the line of the overhead wires, passing a double power pole on your left. Keep straight on through the hedgerow and then along a short stretch between a conifer hedge on the left and a wooden fence on the right.

Turn left at the road. At the junction of lanes by a former chapel keep straight on. About 200 yards past the junction and just after the duck pond, turn right at Highbury Farm. Pass through the farmyard and an iron gate, then turn left, with a hedge on your left and a tree to your right. Head for a gateway near the corner of the field (*see* sketch A). Pass through the gate and then bear right crossing the field diagonally. Aim for a gate in the hedge ahead of you, about halfway along the hedge. Go through the gateway and turn left, with the hedge on your left and the field on your right. Turn right at the corner of the field and proceed with woods on your left. At the next corner turn left, and at the next one, following the edge of the wood, turn right. The path follows the woods downhill. At the bottom of the hill, cross a brick

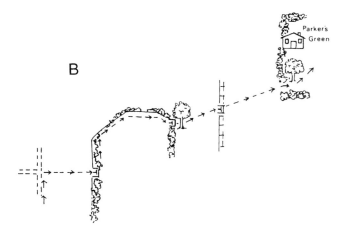

B

Parker's Green

bridge and turn left, with the hedge and trees on your left and the field on your right.

Turn right at the next corner and right again at the corner after that, walking uphill on a surfaced track with the hedge on your left and the field on your right. 10/9 Continue on the track which turns right at the top of the rise, and about 60 yards later turns left, following the line of the hedge. Good views here. When the hedge peters out maintain the same direction going uphill.

At the top of the hill you reach a junction with another bridleway from your left. 9/10 Turn right at this point, to make a continuous straight line with the bridleway that connected on your left. The path crosses an open field here. Head towards the hedgerow across the field and find a gap in the hedge, which will be a few yards to your right (*see* sketch B). Go through the gap across a ditch, turn left and continue with the hedge on your left. Follow the hedge right at the first corner, right again at the next corner, and at the third corner turn left, through a gap in the hedge alongside an ash tree. Head for the gap on the far side of the field close to an oak tree. Maintain the same general direction across the next field, aiming slightly to the right of a power pole which is itself a little to the right of a thatched cottage surrounded by trees. Find a grassy track through the bushes just to the left of an oak tree. Follow that track to the green. Bear right so that you are now walking along the green path. Keep straight on at a junction of paths until the path becomes partly gravel. Continue walking ahead along the track.

The gravel track leads to a gate and a small open space where you will see a red brick bungalow (Blacksmiths) opposite.

Make your way towards the bungalow and turn left onto a track in front of it, so that the bungalow is on your right. Just before the track passes through a metal gateway into a field, turn left onto a green lane which has a ditch on the right and bushes and trees on the left.

You need to walk along this lane* for about 500 yards to a point where it bends to the right. After a few yards, you bear left, ignoring the track ahead. Continue in your original direction along the green lane for another 170 yards and turn sharp right onto another green lane. Continue, with small intermittent lengths of hedge on either side, for about 450 yards, and emerge on to Muncher's Green, just after a track has joined you on your right. Keep straight on across Muncher's Green, veering slightly to the right of a hedge and trees in front of you. At the far side of the green the track that you are following makes a sharp right bend through a wide gateway. Do not follow the track through this gate but keep straight on along a grassy track, passing overgrown ponds on your left. This track can often be quite wet. You can see white houses in the distance as the track emerges onto Moor Green where you started the walk.

---

* This lane is popular with 4 × 4 drivers and can be very muddy. There is a parallel footpath through the fields which may be preferable. If the lane looks bad, it will get worse further on. Return to the open space and go through the gateway into the field on the left of the lane (as viewed from the bungalow).

You enter a narrow field and follow a hedge on your left. After 120 yards the hedge peters out and you continue forward 40 yards to a culvert over a ditch. Then bear slightly right to the corner of the field and go through a gap in the hedge to the next field. Follow the ditch and hedge bordering the green lane on your right for 350 yards to the next corner. Cross a ditch and go through the hedge into the next field. Follow the hedge on your right again for another 150 yards to a point where the field narrows and there is a tree in the hedgerow about 30 yards to your left. Cross a culvert into the green lane on your right and take a narrower green lane opposite. This is the lane which leads to Muncher's Green.

WALK NO. 11

Cottered going South

Cottered – Brook End – Flanders Green – Moor Hall – Cottered Warren Farm – Cottered

Distance 4¹/₄ miles
It is best to park in the cul-de-sac lane that leads to Brook End (GR 323293). (This is the same starting point as Walk No. 12, Cottered going North.)

Cottered recreation ground is alongside the A507 road in the village of Cottered. 11/12 Walk from the phone box along the lane to Brook End. After 350 yards, where the lane bends to the left in front of a thatched cottage (Strawberry Cottage), turn right down an untarred track. Follow the track left around the garden of Strawberry Cottage, passing Flanders Green Cottage on your right.

Facing you is the gable end of a bungalow (Meadow Court). Pass between an outhouse on your left and Meadow Court on your right and turn right towards an open field (*see* sketch A). Cross the stile into the field and bear left towards a corner in the hedge about 220 yards away.

On reaching the corner of the field, go over the stile and turn right along a green lane. This is muddy in places. The lane narrows and becomes more overgrown and then curves fairly sharply to the left. It then becomes a bit wider and crosses a small stream where there is a cottage called The Place on your right-hand side. Continue along the lane (now metalled) for 100 yards until you pass under electricity cables, at which point the lane bends sharply right. At the bend turn half left and leave the lane to go along a track going gradually uphill. Keep on going with the hedge on your left and a post and rail fence on your right (*see* sketch B).

Where the hedge ends, carefully maintain the same direction across

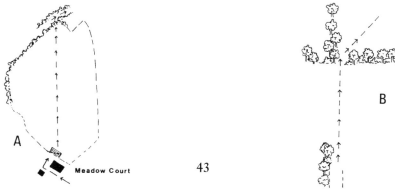

A

Meadow Court

B

the open field towards a hedge. When you reach the far side of the field, find a footbridge close to the point where the low hedge to the left becomes higher to the right. Cross the bridge and turn half right, to cross the next field diagonally, and pass through an area planted with saplings. As you cross this field you gradually converge with the hedgerow on your left. When you meet up with the hedge at the corner turn half right to another footbridge. Cross the bridge to emerge into a field.

Turn left and proceed with the hedge on your left and the field on your right. At the corner of the field cross the footbridge in front of you and turn right, so that you continue with the ditch on your right and the field on your left. This ditch, called The Old Bourne, divides the parishes of Cottered and Aspenden. In centuries past, it was the boundary between the hundreds of Odsey and Edwinstree. You will be crossing and recrossing this ancient boundary as you walk southwards for the next mile.

After following the bourne for 300 yards on your right, cross over a cartbridge into the corner of a field on the other side and continue with The Old Bourne on your left. At the corner of this field pass through the hedge and keep straight ahead onto a path where you have a ditch on both sides. Keep straight on where the path has trees and bushes on either side. The ditches cross your path several times and, in wet weather, you may have to deviate into the fields on your left. When you reach the T-junction of tracks turn right along the old Roman road 'Back Lane'. In a few yards cross The Old Bourne for the last time on a wooden bridge and immediately find a stile on your left. $\boxed{11/10}$.

Turn left to cross the stile and then turn half right, to cross the field diagonally. You go under power cables, pass a power pole on your right and aim for the corner of a wood. Gradually draw nearer to the wood on your left, go through a gateway in a wire fence and bear left alongside the wood. A farmhouse comes into view. Gradually move away from the edge of the wood to aim straight for the farmhouse. Converge with the hedge on your left and go through the gap, which has old wooden gateposts. Continue diagonally across the next field to the right of the lone tree with the farmhouse about 100 yards to your right at your nearest approach to it.

This field has a number of dips in it. You gradually converge on the wire fence and hedge on your right-hand side. Bear right fairly close to the hedge and in the right-hand corner of the field climb over a stile near a new bungalow on your left. Turn left and continue fairly close to the hedge on your left, but to the right of the power pole, and pass under electricity cables to reach a stile onto a track. $\boxed{10/11}$ (If you wish to reach the road at Moor Green turn left along that track.)

To continue to walk back to Cottered, turn sharp right along the track, so that you are now walking directly towards the farmhouse. Just before you reach the farmhouse buildings turn left, so that you proceed with the black farm buildings on your right. Where the farm track

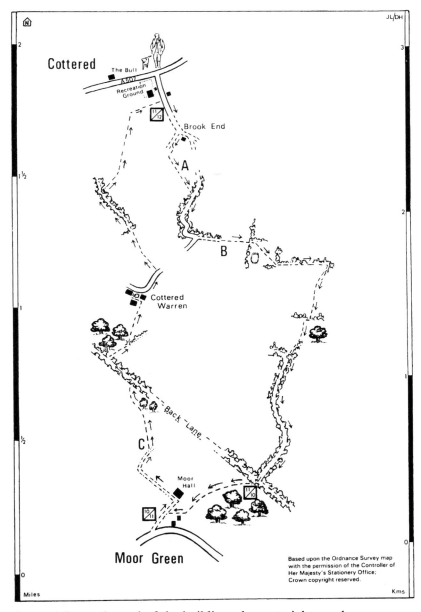

Cottered

The Bull

A507

Recreation Ground

11/½

Brook End

A

B

Cottered Warren

Back Lane

C

Moor Hall

10

10/11

Moor Green

Based upon the Ordnance Survey map with the permission of the Controller of Her Majesty's Stationery Office; Crown copyright reserved.

Miles

Kms

bears right, at the end of the buildings, keep straight on along a grassy path, passing a pond and a clump of bushes on your left.

You are now on a grassy track. You pass a solitary tree on your right and a gate on your left, near where the track makes a right-hand

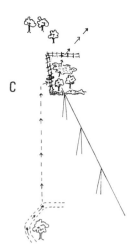

C

bend, and head towards a wood. Approximately halfway between the tree and the wood the track bears to the right again. At that point bear left, across the field, which may be ploughed or have a crop on it. Looking across the field you see power poles (*see* sketch C). You should be about 30 yards to the left of the first pole in the middle of the field, and you must aim about 20 yards to the left of the next pole, that is, towards the corner of a hedgerow jutting into the field. When you reach the corner of the hedge, bear very slightly left and continue for 10 yards with the hedge on your right and the open field on your left. Turn right over a stile and immediately turn left, towards a pond. The path runs straight through the pond to a stile on the other side and, at the time of writing, a causeway is being built across the pond. Pass under electricity wires and cross the stile. Then bear very slightly right, aiming for a stile adjacent to a tree in the boundary hedge, cross that stile and turn left along Back Lane.

Back Lane is wet and muddy in places. Go approximately 300 yards along Back Lane and turn right over a footbridge where woodland starts on your right. After the right turn, you proceed with the wood on your left and a field on your right. Where the wood ends on your left, turn left over a wooden bridge across a ditch, into a field. Cross the field diagonally, aiming for the large building at the right end of the group you can see in the distance. When you are close to the buildings pass the end of the garden fence on your left and turn left across a concrete yard. Pass through a gateway between wooden buildings onto the driveway of Warren Grange. Keep on along a driveway with a laurel hedge on your right out onto the road beside The Lodge on your right.

Turn right along the untarred road following the telephone wires. In a little under 200 yards turn left by some trees at the signpost 'Footpath to Cottered ½'. You are now in an open field. Keep straight on where a ditch crosses and proceed uphill with the hedge on your left and the field on your right. You pass under electricity cables, pass a power pole in the hedge on your left and 40 yards or so after that look out for a gap in the hedge on your left which gives access to a green lane. Turn left through the gap, cross a ditch and then turn right to continue in the same direction, along the green lane.

About 300 yards along the lane just before it bends to the right, look for a stile on the right in the hedge. Cross the stile and aim across the field for the nearest power pole. Pass close to the pole and maintain the same direction. You pass under another set of cables aiming for a tree in the corner ahead. Cross a small concrete bridge and a stile, and continue in the same general direction towards another stile you can see in the wire fence on the right-hand side of the field. Cross that stile and keep on going the same way. Cross a wooden stile in the next hedge, turn right and immediately cross some iron railings into Cottered recreation ground from where the walk commenced. 11/12

Cottered Church Doors — Aylott 1907

WALK NO. 12

Cottered going North

Cottered – Broadfield Hall – Whitehall Farm – Coles Green – Cottered

Distance 5¹/₂ miles

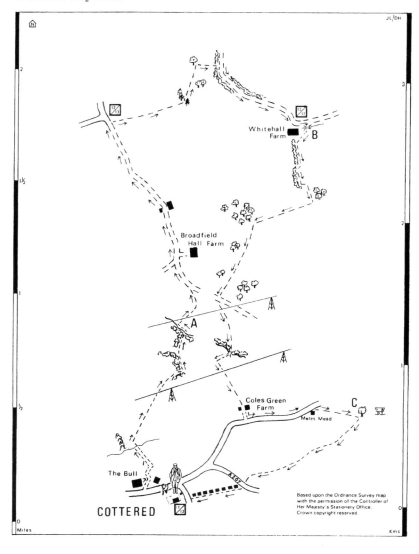

It is best to park in the cul-de-sac lane that leads to Brook End (GR 323293). (This is the same starting point as Walk No. 11, Cottered going South.)

This is another walk from Cottered Recreation Ground which is on the southern side of the A507 in the village. 11/12

Cross the A507 and turn left. At the Bull public house turn right along a track beside the pub so that you pass the pub on your left with Glebe House on your right. You pass a signpost 'Public Bridleway to Broadfield Hall 1¼' and 10 yards on there is a turning to the right but you must keep straight on past an electricity sub-station on your left. The track now turns to the right along the edge of an open field. Follow it and in 40 yards turn left at the field corner. You have a hedge on the right and the track goes gradually downhill until you cross a stream (sometimes dried up) and emerge into a large field.

The field is crossed by two parallel rows of high-tension cables. Turn to your right, so that you cross the field diagonally, going gradually uphill, aiming to the left of the pylon which is on the right of the field. You gradually converge with the high-tension cables to your left and pass the pylon about 15 yards to your right. About 60 yards ahead you reach the corner of a hedge, and you continue with the hedge on your right and the field on your left. After another 60 yards when you reach the corner of the field do not turn left or right but make your way through the bushes (there is a gap) in front of you.

Cross a ditch and when you emerge into the next field turn left. Continue with a hedge on your left and the field on your right. Where the hedge curves to the left leave the hedgerow and bear slightly right across 70 yards of open field to the right end of a spinney on the other side. Turn right, so that you continue in the same field with the hedge on your left and the field on your right. When you reach the far corner of the field make your way through the bushes and trees ahead of you to a bridge. When you emerge into the field on the far side turn left. Continue with a ditch and hedge on your left and the field on your right. You will see a tall pylon in this field. When you reach the point where the hedge on your left ends and only the ditch continues, that is before you reach the overhead cables, turn right across the field (*see* sketch A).

Aiming for the wooden power pole nearest the pylon, you pass diagonally under the cables and pass the pylon about 60 yards to your right. When you reach the power pole turn half left in the field and aim for a tree to the right of the next power pole. You emerge at a bend on a metalled road, and there you turn left. You keep on this road in the same direction for a little more than three quarters of a mile, passing Broadfield Hall Farm and Lodge Farm on your right and, further on, reaching a section where the road has a concrete surface and there are farm buildings on either side.

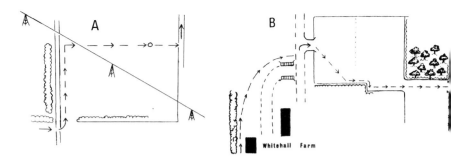

After that concrete section keep straight on uphill, where you have a bungalow and then a brick house to your right. As you are going up the hill you will see ahead of you a junction of lanes with a signpost pointing to Rushden. Twenty yards before you reach the junction of lanes you will find an indentation in the bank on the right-hand side.

12/13

Turn right there, off the road, and set off to cross two large fields. Crossing the first field, you see ahead a line of trees, and you aim for the right-hand end of that line, where you will find an earth bridge over a ditch. Cross the ditch and continue uphill across the next field in the same direction.

At the top of the hill you will see a line of broadleaf trees to the left and a line of conifers to the right. Aim for a point inside the conifer plantation just to the right of the last tall oak tree. At that point, cross the ditch, and make your way through the trees in front of you.

Bear left, picking out the best route between the trees, and in a few yards you reach a field. You cross the field diagonally, gradually leaving the line of trees on your left (*see* sketch B for Walk 13). Looking across the field you can see the point where the line of trees and bushes to your left comes to an end. Aim for that point, and as you cross the field you pass within 25 yards of a pond, surrounded by bushes, to your right. When you reach the point aimed for, you will find a ditch with an earth bridge. Do not cross the bridge but turn right, so that you continue with a ditch on your left and the field on your right. When you reach the corner of the field, find a way through the clump of bushes in front of you, cross a footbridge, and then turn right along a track. The track goes downhill, and in 70 yards you turn left, on a grassy track with a ditch on your left and the field on your right. Cross a stile beside a field-gate into another field and continue with the ditch on your left. At the corner of this field, cross a stile into another field where you see farm machinery. 13/12 You pass a newish bungalow on your right (*see* sketch B). The path curves round through an old orchard to the farm entrance with a low brick wall on your right. Turn left on to a concrete track, and in 40 yards turn right, over a ditch into a field.

Cross this field diagonally to a point on the far side about 150 yards away. Once there, follow the hedge on your right uphill towards the right end of a wood on the horizon. At the corner of the field pass through the gap, to continue with the wood on your left and another field on your right. At the next corner of the wood turn right and follow a shallow ditch on your left between open fields.

Where the ditch makes a right turn across your path, continue straight on across an open piece of field, aiming for a point where Great Wood ahead becomes a row of trees and bushes. When you reach the far side of the field, go through the gap in the hedge and emerge into the next field.

There you will have the wood on your right. Turn half left to cross the field diagonally. In the fields beyond there are high-tension cables, and you will be aiming for a point where the cables are at their lowest, midway between pylons. As you proceed you pass a large clump of trees just a few yards to your right. Still maintaining a straight line, continue down a dip, passing near a small woodland on your left.

Keeping parallel with the wood on your left, as you go uphill you will pass through a field-gate in a post and rail fence approaching the high-tension cables ahead. You do not cross them in this field.

At the next gate, you cross a metalled road and enter the field opposite under the lowest point of the cables. Cross the field diagonally, well to the right of a wooden power pole. Aim for a point in the hedge opposite where the row of tall trees to the right gives way to lower bushes to the left. When you reach the hedgerow, turn right to cross the footbridge, which is hidden in the hedge.

At the next field go straight ahead for 125 yards, aiming slightly to the right of a pylon. When you are halfway to the pylon turn left. The ground rises ahead and as you get to the top pass under the power cables across your route. Ahead you will see an iron gate leading to a farm to the left of a metal barn. Pass through the gate and then between the buildings of Coles Green Farm and soon after reach the road.

To shorten the walk, you can turn right here, to walk down the road to where it meets the main road. This is the A507. Turn right (towards Cromer), and walk the remaining half mile along the footway to return to the start of the walk.

To continue on the full route, which is about a half mile longer, turn left outside Coles Green Farm along the road past Whitegates Farm to a point where the road bears left and on the right is a house, Moles Mead. Fork right there through the wooden gate (not the gate to the house), and cross the field diagonally, aiming for the furthermost corner, where there is a clump of trees.

Pass the trees on your right into the next field. Continue in the same direction across this field, aiming for the large oak tree ahead (*see* sketch

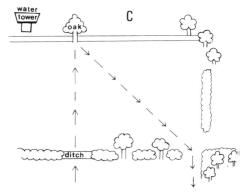

C). There you will find a ditch and you are in line with a water tower further to your left.

Here you virtually about-turn to your right, and cross the same field again, but aiming for the field corner opposite. This is the corner that was 90 degrees to your right when you first entered this field.

At this corner of the field bear slightly right over an earth bridge into the field ahead. (The left abutment of the bridge bears an inscription in the concrete '2 AUSTRIA P.O.W. 20 II 1946'). Head straight across the open field to the nearest corner of the hedgerow about 400 yards away. Pass through this corner and continue in the same direction with the hedge on your right.

Where the hedge curves to the right, leave the line of the hedge and cross the field, aiming to the left of the houses and straight towards a power pole. Cross the road and continue with hedge and houses on the right. At the corner of the field, bear right by a field-gate then left, down a garage drive. At the lane turn right. You will then see the telephone box just off the A507 at Cottered. Turn left to return to the recreation ground. 11/12

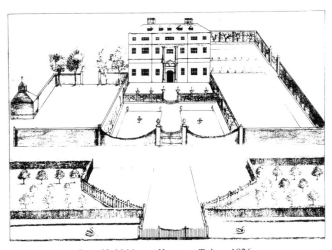

Broadfield Manor House — Tyler c.1826

WALK NO. 13

Sandon going South

Sandon – Beckfield Farm – Mill End – Whitehall Farm – Roe Green – Sandon

Distance 5 miles

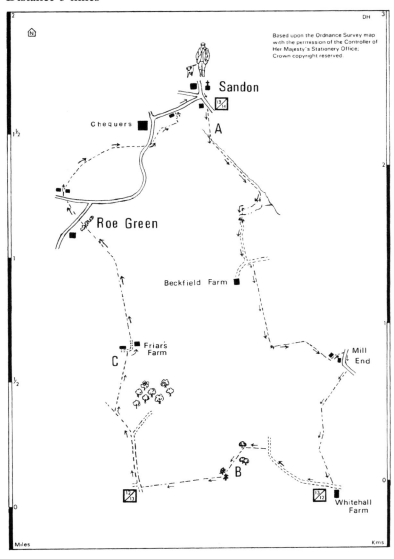

Based upon the Ordnance Survey map with the permission of the Controller of Her Majesty's Stationery Office; Crown copyright reserved.

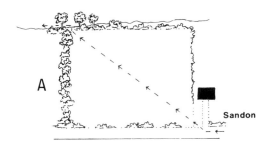

A

Sandon

There is usually room to park near the church or alternatively on the triangle of lanes that serve the village (GR 322344).

The walk starts on the road outside the church.

Walk south towards the signpost and take the lane towards Buckland and Buntingford. 13/14 In a few yards, at a point where there are farm buildings on your left, you will see a house to your right. Take the rough track which leads towards the left-hand side of this house (*see* sketch A). When you enter the field bear slightly left and cross the field diagonally, aiming downhill to the furthermost corner, where there are some poplar trees. At the corner of the field cross the ditch in front of you and turn left. You continue with the hedge and ditch on your left and the open field on your right. Keep to the edge of the field, as it makes several bends following the line of the ditch, ignoring the footbridges to your left.

When you reach the corner of the field turn right, going uphill, with a hedge on your left and the field on your right. Pass a stile on your left and continue uphill. Pass under electricity wires and a few yards after that you will find a second stile on your left, at a point where the hedge makes a 90 degree turn to the right. (You may have to penetrate stinging nettles to reach it.) Cross the stile which takes you into the adjacent field, keeping the hedge on your right and the field on your left. In a few yards you will cross a ditch and, a few yards further on at the corner, find a gate in the hedge on your right.

Go through the gate, remembering to close it behind you, and then immediately turn left. In this field you go uphill slightly, with the hedge on your left. The path soon takes a right bend, then a left bend, and you continue to have the hedge on your left. You will be walking towards some farm buildings. You eventually cross a stile onto a narrow lane and turn left. In about 40 yards, at the next telegraph pole, turn right into a large field with a paddock on your right. Continue with a wooden fence on your right and the field on your left. Where the fence on your right ceases, keep straight on across the open field. As you progress aim for the right-hand end of the line of trees ahead. When you reach a fence on your left-hand side, continue in approximately the same direction, following the line of the fence on your left.

You will be going downhill to the corner of the field and there turn left, over a stile. Follow the ditch on your right. In a few yards you come to a gateway on your right. Go through the gateway and turn left over a stile. Pass through a small spinney to a footbridge. Cross the bridge and follow the ditch on your left to a second stile. Cross this and a third stile a few yards further on on your right into a large field. Once in the field, take the right-hand one of the two paths which cross this field uphill towards the right end of a post and rail fence. Aim for a field-gate near the end of the fence.

When you reach the brow of the hill go through the gate into a paddock and cross to the opposite corner, passing a low building on your left. Cross a stile just beyond it. Continue in the same direction and in a few yards you will find the entrance to a short narrow path, enclosed by overhanging branches. You emerge onto a lane and turn right.

Go uphill along the road for about 100 yards and then turn right at the footpath just before the next group of buildings. This is usually a well-defined track going uphill with an electrified fence on the left. At the brow of this minor hill, turn left with the fence and a sparse hedge on a bank. Go downhill, with the bank on your left and the field on your right. At the corner of this field you cross a ditch and an electrified fence into the next field. Look down the hill in line with the hedge on your left towards some farm buildings. Aim for the long single-storey building you see in front of you below a pylon on the skyline.

When you reach the far side of the field, cross a stile, and turn right in front of the bungalow. (There may be some wooden barriers you will have to cross.) Go through an enclosure where farm machinery is parked keeping to the hedge on your right. $\boxed{13/12}$ You will be going gradually uphill away from the farm, over a stile beside a field-gate onto a grassy track. The track makes a number of curves, and eventually takes a right turn, which you also take, going a little more steeply uphill. There will now be a ditch and hedge on your left. About 70 yards after the right turn, turn left over a bridge to emerge into a field where you have a ditch on your right and the field on your left.

The ditch on your right eventually enters a culvert (see sketch B) and you come to a clump of bushes and trees. Turn half left, crossing an open field, which is often ploughed or has a crop on it. You pass close to a small pond surrounded by a clump of bushes about 20 yards to your left as you cross the field. You should be aiming towards the right end of a small plantation of fir trees to the left of a tall oak about 150 yards beyond the pond. When you reach the plantation make your way through the trees, maintaining the same direction until you can see the opening on your right into the adjacent field, about 10 yards past the oak tree.

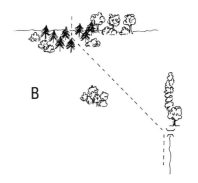

B

From the opening, aim straight across the field, leaving the hedgerow directly behind you. As you cross the field, at the point where it slopes downwards you will see that there is a hedgerow, which has some tall trees. Aim for the left end of the tall trees. When you reach that point, you will see that there is an earth bridge over a ditch, which you cross. Keep on in the same direction towards the left end of a row of conifer trees. On the far side of the field you emerge onto a lane and turn right. 12/13 A few yards on, at the junction of lanes, keep straight on signposted 'Wood Farm Only'. When you reach the junction of tracks where the concrete track turns to the right, keep straight on, along a grassy track, thus leaving the lane with the made-up surface. About 60 yards along the grassy track you emerge into a field, where you bear left, along the boundary of a field, so that you have a ditch and hedge to your left.

As you proceed keep a watch on the ditch to your left, until you reach a point where there is a junction of ditches and hedgerows. About 20 yards further on, turn right, away from the ditch and hedge, to cross the open field. On the skyline you will see a long bungalow and you aim just to the right of this (*see* sketch C). Close to the bungalow you cross a paddock by way of two stiles and emerge onto a gravel drive, which bears right a few yards along, to bring you close to the outbuildings of a house on your right. Turn left, to pass between

C

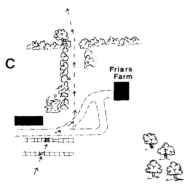

the long bungalow and the outbuildings of the house. Keep left, leaving the path, and proceed along a grassy area with a hedge on your left and a raised lawn on your right.

At the point where the hedge ceases there is an ash tree and you emerge into a large field. Maintaining the same general direction, go out into the field. The field is crossed by two ditches. The first ditch runs only part-way across the field from your left and you should pass close to its right-hand end. You will now be able to see overhead power lines ahead to your left. You must look for the pole with a guy rope and double insulators where the cables slightly change direction. A little to the right of the pole is a bridge across the second ditch, by a small tree. Cross the ditch and head towards a lone tree in the open field. Pass under the power lines. About half-way between the power lines and the tree, you have to bear slightly left at a junction with another path which may or may not be visible on the ground. Look in the distance for a gap in the far hedge. You may be able to pick out the white goal-posts in the recreation ground beyond the hedge, and beyond those the gable-end of a light-coloured house. Continue across the field, aiming for these landmarks.

Pass through the gap in the hedge onto Roe Green and maintain the same direction. Cross a road, and soon after that pass in front of the sports pavilion. Proceed across the green to the left of the cricket square to reach another road. Across the road is a dwelling known as Tay House whose gable-end faces you and which has an area of bushes and a small pond to its left. You need to find the footpath at the back of the pond. You reach it through the bushes to the left of Tay House.

Behind the pond you will find a notice which tells you that you are now on the Icknield Way Path (*see* note at end of Walk 14) and a stile. Cross the stile, and continue into the field with a shallow pond on your left and a line of small trees and a fence on your right. There is a fence directly ahead of you with a stile at the right-hand end. Cross this and continue into the next field. Keep straight ahead across more stiles, aiming towards an ancient oak, just beyond which you will see a gate with a stile alongside. Cross the stile and bear very slightly right. You will gradually converge with the fence and hedge on your right. At a dog-leg in the wooden fencing, cross a stile and a ditch and a second stile to reach the adjacent field. Bearing very slightly left as you go uphill towards a thatched cottage and two other buildings, you again gradually converge with the fence and hedge, this time on your left, until you reach the gate at the corner. Cross a stile onto the road and turn left.

After 20 yards turn right and, after crossing a stile, turn left. You proceed with the remains of a hedge on your right and just a little way from a hedge by the road on your left. When the hedge on your right ceases, keep straight on across the small field. A slight detour to your left takes you to the Chequers public house but your route lies towards

57

the wire fence on your right. In the far right corner of the field find a piece of wooden fencing and, just beyond, a gateway in an iron railing fence. Go through the gate into the playing field of the school. Skirt round the field, keeping the iron railings on your right and the school on your left. Eventually, when you reach the kissing-gate on the far side of the playing field, turn through this gate and immediately turn left, and continue with the railings on your left. Cross a small stile and pass between some wooden sheds and the iron railings. You pass close to a house on your right which is the village store and Post Office. Keep ahead to the road and turn right, back to the start of the walk.

Monumental Brasses, Sandon Church

WALK NO. 14

Therfield going South

Therfield – Kelshall – Sandon – Therfield

Distance 5 miles

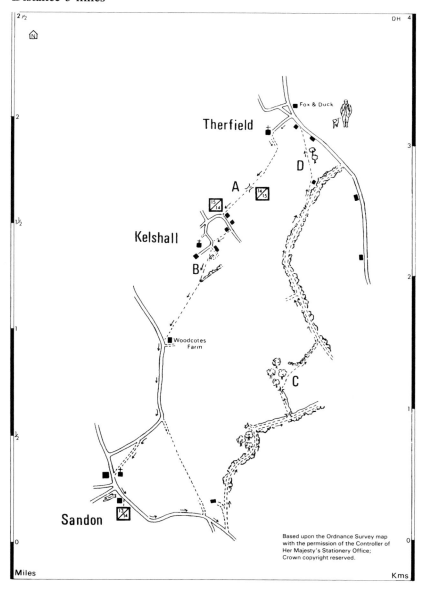

Based upon the Ordnance Survey map with the permission of the Controller of Her Majesty's Stationery Office; Crown copyright reserved.

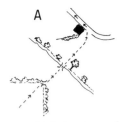

A

There is usually room to park near the village green which is situated opposite the Fox and Duck public house (GR 336372).

This walk starts from Therfield village green. Walk directly away from the Fox and Duck across the road. Pass the wooden Therfield sign and continue down Church Lane.

Walk towards the church and enter the churchyard. Pass the church on your right. As you are passing the church turn left, so that you go through a gap in some iron railings and away from the church. You are now on a grassy track, with railings and a house on your left and a field and hedgerow on your right. When the track reaches the next field turn half right, to cross the field diagonally, aiming for the furthermost corner, where you see a power pole. At that corner you will find a small earth bridge over a ditch, and an old broken gateway, which takes you into the next field.

You now face a large open field which you must cross in approximately the same direction as you have been travelling. On the distant horizon you see houses, and where a clump of trees rises higher than the houses you may be able to see the top of Kelshall Church tower. Aim straight for that. To get across the ditch running through the field, look for a small solitary tree with two power poles to the right of it (*see* sketch A). Your route should take you a little to the left of that tree. When you reach this point you will find there is a wide earth bridge over the ditch. 14/15 Maintain the same direction and pass under two sets of electricity wires and gradually approach a house which has gable ends. About 20 yards to the right of the house you meet a lane 15/14 and there turn left, to pass in front of the house. Pass another house on the left called The Maltings (which has a civic award) and, just beyond a new bungalow on your right, turn right onto a public footpath.

You now have a hedge and bungalow on your right and field on your left. Where the hedge on your right ends continue across the open field, aiming just to the right of some trees on the right of a row of timber-clad houses. On the far side of the field you will find a gap in the hedge, which leads onto a lane. Turn left along the lane and follow it around a bend to the right. You pass one of the timber-clad houses and

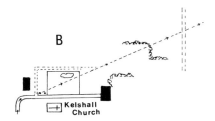

B

Kelshall
Church

outbuildings on your left and as soon as you have passed them fork left, so that you go just to the left of a telegraph pole (*see* sketch B).

At this point the land crossed by the footpath has been fenced off to make a garden but stiles have been provided. Cross the timber fence and enter an area of well-trimmed grass and continue in the same direction, moving gradually away from the lane and the church, which are to your right. You pass a pond on your left just before you reach a second timber fence. Cross that and proceed in the same direction, to cross a small field diagonally, aiming for the far corner. As you proceed you pass within 50 yards of the corner of a hedge on your right. You gradually converge with a hedge to your left and aim for a clump of trees, where there is a stile. Cross the stile and continue in the same direction. Ahead is a large field which rises towards some farm buildings on the skyline. Aim just to the right of those buildings.

Part-way across the field you cross the track of a bridleway. Good views here. Continue to aim to the right of the farm buildings, towards the corner made by two hedgerows which should now be clearly visible. Pass by a tree and over a ditch onto a road. Turn left along the road and pass in front of the farmhouse. After half a mile the road bends to the right. Two hundred yards beyond the bend, at the 'Sandon' sign, take the footpath on the left uphill along a narrow path with hedges on both sides. You may meet some Icknield Wayfarers on this path, probably travelling in the opposite direction to you. You emerge into the churchyard, passing the church on your left. Pass through the lychgate onto the road and turn left. 13/14 At the road junction keep straight on in the direction signposted 'Buckland and Buntingford'.

In just over half a mile fork left at a road junction, turning left after about 50 yards along the drive to a house where you will have a green on your left and bushes and woods to your right. You are now back on the Icknield Way Path travelling in the popular direction. Just before the house fork right, on a rougher path uphill through woods. This is a very wet and muddy lane. Eventually you have woodland on your left and further on the lane does a right turn. Turn right there to stay on the path, do not go through the gate to your left. Continue with bushes on both sides.

Four hundred yards after the right bend, turn left through the bushes to a wooden bridge, leaving the Icknield Way Path. Cross the ditch, and continue with the field on your left and another ditch on your right. You are walking towards a small wood. When you reach the corner of the field at the edge of the wood turn right, crossing an earth bridge over the ditch. You continue with the wood on your left and the field on your right for about 80 yards but, at the point where the boundary of the wood makes a right-angled turn to the left, proceed across the open field, maintaining your previous direction (*see* sketch C).

As you are heading towards a row of medium-sized trees on the far side of the field you will meet up with a hedgerow where it makes a bend. There continue downhill with an open field on your right and the hedge on your left. At the corner of the field, turn left along a muddy grass lane which is the Icknield Way Path again. You stay with this well-used route as far as Therfield. It continues as a wide gravel track between hedges and ditches.

At the point where the main track makes a turn to the left you go straight on, leaving the gravel track, and continuing on a muddy lane with a thick hedge on the left and a sparse hedge and bank on the right. This lane is very muddy in patches and winds gradually uphill with trees and bushes on both sides. After 300 yards, the lane bends slightly to the right and then starts to broaden out. You reach a point where power lines cross overhead and, looking across the field to your right you see farm buildings and houses while in the field on your left you see a power pole. Ignore the first path to your left, which you pass about 100 yards after the power lines, and press on along the lane for another 200 yards where you will find an iron gate and a stile on your left leading into a pasture field.

Turn left over the stile and then immediately right, aiming for the far corner of the field (*see* sketch D). Pass through the hedge at the corner where a stile has been provided, and in the next field continue in approximately the same direction towards a gate. You pass under electricity cables and then through the gateway. In the next field turn slightly left. You aim towards a large tree beyond which, slightly to the right, is a house about 300 yards from where you entered the field. As you proceed you gradually move further away from the electricity cables which you see to your left. The path follows the line of a slight indentation in the field and has a number of old trees along it. Keep straight on and pass the house on your right, where you have a hedge on your right and the field on your left. At the corner of the field you cross a stile and continue past a double power pole over a grassy area to the road.

When you reach the road turn left, to return to the village green.

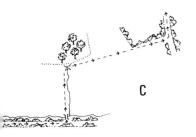

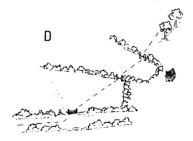

The Icknield Way is unique among long distance tracks because it can claim to be 'the oldest road in Britain'. It consists of prehistoric pathways, ancient when the Romans came; the route is dotted with archaeological remains. It survives today in splendid tracks and green lanes along the chalk 'spine' of southern England.

The Icknield Way Path takes the walker over some delightful country, often with striking panoramic views, through some charming villages, and along miles of beautiful 'green lanes'. It runs a distance of something over 100 miles through six counties from Ivinghoe Beacon to the southern end of the Peddars Way near Thetford. The Icknield Way Association has worked since 1984 to devise this walkers' route and to obtain official recognition of it.

The designation of the Icknield Way Path as a Regional Recreational Route has led to its being signposted and waymarked throughout, and to a large number of other improvements carried out by the six County Councils. It was officially opened by the Chairman of the Countryside Commission at a happy and well-attended ceremony at Balsham on 11 September 1992.

For more information, contact:

> Roy Wheeler
> Membership Secretary
> Icknield Way Association
> 19 Boundary Road
> BISHOPS STORTFORD
> CM23 5LE

WALK NO. 15

Ashwell Station to Therfield

Ashwell and Morden Station – Gallows Hill – Stumps Cross – Kelshall – Therfield – Ashwell and Morden Station

Distance 6½ miles

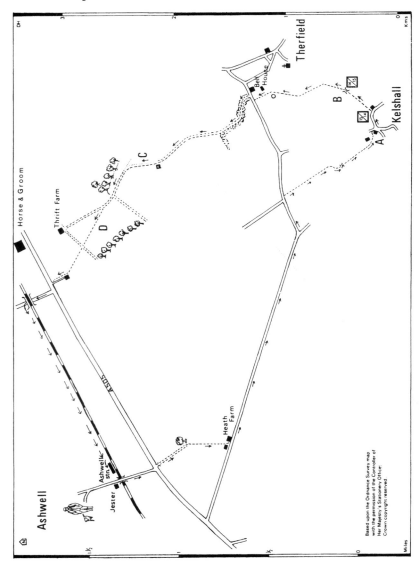

There is a car park at Ashwell and Morden Station and it is also possible to park in the road, preferably to the north of the station.

This walk starts from Ashwell and Morden Station. The station is in Cambridgeshire, although the village of Ashwell is in Hertfordshire.

Walk south along the road from the station, using the pathway which runs along the right-hand side of the road. After passing the Jester public house you reach an intersection with a dual carriageway road (A505). Go straight on here, crossing the main road carefully, and enter the field opposite, using a path which crosses a ditch on an earth bridge. Go uphill towards a clump of trees; there are good views from the top of this hill (Gallows Hill). Pass the trees on your left and proceed downhill towards some farm buildings. Keep straight on across a lawn, between a bungalow on your right and the farm buildings to your left, then onto a road, where you turn left.

Regrettably, there is a fair amount of road on this walk and you now start the longest section of it. Continue steadily uphill on the road for a mile or so, taking an occasional look back at the view across Cambridgeshire. At the road junction turn left, where there is a signpost to Therfield. There is now a good long-distance view to your left. At the next junction, where a lane joins from your left, keep straight on for about 60 yards, then turn onto a footpath on your right. You climb a low bank and then proceed along the edge of a field, with an open field on your right and, a little later, a hedge on your left.

Further on the path goes downhill. At the bottom of this hill, where there is a corner, turn right for a few yards and then left, to follow the line of the ditch and hedge on your left once more. In a few more yards you cross a ditch by an earth bridge, where there is usually an abundance of stinging nettles. Continue in the same direction uphill, still with the hedge on your left. Where the hedge ends, about 70 yards after the earth bridge, cross a stile and keep straight on uphill across the open field. Pass to the left of a solitary tree to two stiles in the fence ahead of you. Cross these stiles and continue in the same direction across the next field, aiming for another stile to the left of a field-gate.

Just after this stile you will see a gravel track and some farm buildings on your left (*see* sketch A). Cross the track and another stile 30 yards from the last one, then turn left in a grassy area, where there is usually some farm machinery. In about 60 yards you reach yet another stile, which is in a fence. Cross this stile and enter a small field where you should see a power pole about 20 yards to your right, a modern bungalow ahead of you and some older buildings slightly to the right of that. Aim for a point on the far side of the field between the bungalow and the older buildings where there is a hand-gate and emerge by more stiles onto a road close to a road junction.

Go straight along the road ahead of you signposted 'Kelshall Street'. This takes you downhill past a 'No Through Road' traffic sign to your

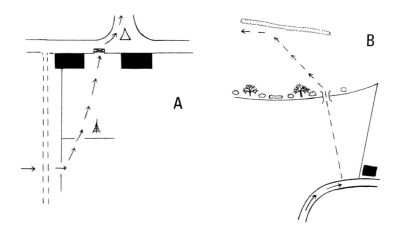

right. As you approach the first house on the left (Haggers Farm), the road curves to the right and just before you reach this house you turn left into a field. 15/14 The path does not go along the edge of the field but follows a route bearing slightly away from the right-hand edge across the field and is not easy to find (*see* sketch B). Looking across the field, you can see Therfield Church and, to the right of the church, the roof of a large house behind some trees. Aim for the point midway between the church and the house.

As you proceed you will pass under two sets of electricity cables. Ahead of you is a ditch, with the remains of a hedge alongside it. You should cross the ditch over an earth bridge, near the right end of the hedge. 14/15 After the bridge take the left fork in the path, aiming for a point between the church and the water tower to its left. When you reach the hedge on the far side of the field turn left, so you follow the edge of the next field with the hedge on your left. At the corner of the field, go through a patchy hedge into another field.

You can now see the water tower clearly. Aiming just to the right of it, cross the field diagonally. Near the tower some allotments cause a small unofficial diversion: turn right, then left, onto a well-defined track and proceed along it, passing the water tower on your left. Further on there is a large thatched building (Tuthill Manor) on your right, which is well worth a look. Eventually you reach a road where you turn right; there are good views across Cambridgeshire from here.

At the bottom of a dip in the road you will find a narrow path between some bushes on your left. Turn left down this path. Should you reach Bell House, you have come too far along the road and will

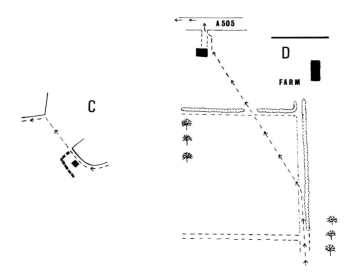

have to retrace your steps for a few yards back to the footpath, which is just to the west of this former public house.

Follow the path, which has an overgrown hedge on each side, for 40 yards to a point where there is a gate ahead and a pond on your right. Turn left here. The path goes gradually downhill. There are still hedges on both sides, it is often overgrown with nettles and brambles and some parts may be muddy. Eventually you emerge at the corner of a field and here you must continue in the same direction, following the hedge on your left. Curve gently to the right, following the line of the hedge, and continue this slightly curving route across the open field when the hedge ends. You will be aiming for the lowest point in a large bowl formed by the contours of this prairie-like field.

As you proceed, the land on your right gradually becomes higher than the path, which now begins to curve to the left, heading towards a small escarpment with bushes growing along it. As you near the escarpment the path curves a little more to the left. You now continue along a grassy track with the field on your left and the rising bank on your right. Further on, the track takes a bend to the right, to follow the line of the bank on your right. Just after this, there is a shooting range on your left. Maintain the same direction across the field to reach another small escarpment where you make a slight left turn, and continue with a fence on your right (*see* sketch C).

Beyond the bank on your right make a note of a clump of trees further up the hill. On your left, at this point, there is usually a farm track, which leads to the end of a line of trees. From this spot go straight on for another 100 yards, then fork left off the track, to cross

67

the open field diagonally (*see* sketch D). You will see a gap in the hedge ahead of you and beyond that a cottage to the right of a larger brick house which is screened by conifers. Line up with the gap and the cottage so that you can keep a straight line as you cross the field. The line of the path goes down a dip, then rises, and you will see farm buildings over to your right. Cross a farm track and then through the gap in the hedge. Maintain the same direction in the next field, aiming for the right side of the cottage. (This field may be sub-divided into livestock enclosures.) Near the cottage you cross a fence onto a lawn and proceed so that you pass close to the cottage on your left. Go up the driveway to the main road (A505).

On reaching this dual carriageway, cross to the central reservation and then, 10 yards to the left, cross the other carriageway to a tarmac road signposted 'Morden Grange Farm Only'.

Pass under the railway bridge ahead of you, then turn immediately left to walk with the railway embankment on your left and open fields to the right. Carry on until you reach quarry workings on the right and, immediately after meeting the haul road to the quarry, veer to the left and pass through a gap to the left of a wide iron gate.

Continue following the railway line through the crane yard and past the station buildings of Ashwell and Morden station, to reach the road and the Jester public house.

Kelshall Church Cross

68

COUNTRYSIDE ACCESS CHARTER

Your rights of way are:
- public footpaths – on foot only;
- bridleways – on foot, horseback and pedal cycle;
- byways (usually old roads), most 'roads used as public paths' and, of course, public roads – all traffic.

Use maps and signs – Ordnance Survey Pathfinder and Landranger maps show most public rights of way – or look for paths that have coloured waymarking arrows – yellow on footpaths, blue on bridleways, red on tracks that can be legally used by vehicles.

On rights of way you can:
- take a pram, pushchair or wheelchair if practicable;
- take a dog (on a lead or under close control);
- take a short route round an illegal obstruction or remove it sufficiently to get past.

You have a right to go for recreation to:
- public parks and open spaces – on foot;
- most commons near older towns and cities – on foot and sometimes on horseback;
- private land where the owner has a formal agreement with the local authority.

In addition
you can *use* the following by local or established *custom or consent* – ask for advice if you're unsure;
- many areas of open country like mountain, moorland, fell and coastal areas, especially those of the National Trust, and most commons;
- some woods and forests, especially those owned by the Forestry Commission;
- country parks and picnic sites;
- most beaches;
- towpaths on canals and rivers;
- some land that is being rested from agriculture, where notices allowing access are displayed;
- some private paths and tracks.

Consent sometimes extends to riding horses and pedal cycles.

For your information
- county and metropolitan district councils and London boroughs have a duty to protect, maintain and record rights of way, and hold registers of commons and village greens – report problems you find to them;
- obstructions, dangerous animals, harassment and misleading signs on rights of way are illegal;
- if a public path runs along the edge of a field, it must not be ploughed or disturbed;
- a public path across a field can be ploughed or disturbed to cultivate a crop, but the surface must be quickly restored and the line of the path made apparent on the ground;
- crops (other than grass) must not be allowed to inconvenience the use of a right of way, or prevent the line from being apparent on the ground;
- landowners can require you to leave land to which you have no right of access;
- motor vehicles are normally permitted only on roads, byways and some 'roads used as public paths';
- follow any local bylaws.

And, wherever you go, follow the country code
Enjoy the countryside and respect its life and work
Guard against all risk of fire
Fasten all gates
Keep your dogs under close control
Keep to public paths across farmland
Use gates and stiles to cross fences, hedges and walls
Leave livestock, crops and machinery alone
Take your litter home
Help to keep all water clean
Protect wildlife, plants and trees
Take special care on country roads
Make no unnecessary noise
This Charter is for practical guidance in England only. More advice is given in a free booklet Out in the country *available from Countryside Commission Postal Sales, PO Box 124, Walgrave, Northampton NN6 9TL.*

© Countryside Commission 1992